PROPHETIC ACCELERATOR II

for Marketplace leaders

Discerning & Deciphering Prophetic Algorithms
(Pslam 139)

Coaching Entrepreneurs, Small Business Leaders and Busy Professionals to Manifest the Prophetic Ministry in the Marketplace

Dr. Joel C. Garcia, P.h.D

PROPHETIC ACCELERATOR II

Discerning & Deciphering Prophetic Algorithms

Published 2024

International Standard Book Number

ISBN: 978-1-963329-68-1

Printed in the United States, 2024, USA

Workbook $20.00

Prophetic Themes in this Workbook

"Then the disciples came to Jesus and asked,

'Why do You speak to the people in parables?'

Jesus replied,

'The knowledge of the mysteries of the kingdom of heaven

has been given to you, but not to them.

Whoever has will be given more, and he will have an abundance.'"

— Matthew 13:11-12 (BSB)

"But, as it is written,

'What no eye has seen, nor ear heard, nor the heart of man

imagined, what God has prepared for those who love him —

these things God has revealed to us through the Spirit.

For the Spirit searches everything, even the depths of God.'"

— 1 Corinthians 2:9-10 (ESV)

Table of Contents

ICON TABLE

God is Omniscient

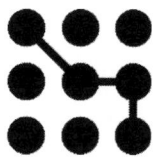

Patterns, Repetitions & Sequences

God is Omnipresent

Past, Present & Future

God is Omnivident

Nocturnal Vision

Prophetic Algorithm

Discerning & Deciphering

Multi-Sensory

Multi-Dimensional

KEY DEFINITIONS OF TERMINOLOGY

DISCERNING

to perceive and to recognize something

DECIPHERING

to succeed in understanding and interpreting
something

PROPHETIC

relating to the flow of prophecy

ALGORITHMS

the multi-dimensional and multi-sensory language of God's
prophetic intent to a recipient

Introduction

The Prophetic Accelerator course will introduce students to a new concept we have dubbed as a *"Prophetic Algorithm"* into the mainstream vocabulary of the prophetic lexicon. The inception of this workbook began when I (Joel) was preparing to deliver a teaching at a prophetic workshop scheduled for February of 2023. Over a month of study, God opened my eyes and unveiled Psalm 139 to me in a whole different light. In the Psalm, King David introduces the reader to a magnificent and multi-faceted God who manifests Himself in three distinct ways. These three characteristics of God's nature are:

1. God is Omniscient: He is all—knowing, Psalm 139:1-6

2. God is Omnipresent: He is always—present, Psalm 139:7-10

3. God is Omnivident: He is all—seeing, Psalm 139:11-18

It is crucial to know God through these three attributes of His divine nature because by knowing God's true substance, we are able to discover our own prophetic identity so we can learn how to walk out our prophetic destiny. David could capture the prophetic algorithms of God's desires for his life, manifesting all God had predestined for his life. You too can manifest what is written about you in the eternal book referenced in Psalm 139 by taking the time to know Him intimately, as David did.

The Psalm itself has a depth of revelation, compelling the reader to dive deeper into the heart and mind of this multi-faceted God. After David reveals the true substance of God's nature, he then takes a sudden turn in verse nineteen. It's quite odd, to say the least, when all of a sudden, the Psalm diverts into a warfare theme: "Oh, that you would slay the wicked, O God! Depart from me, you bloodthirsty men." This personal revelation of David's life purpose is quite a departure from the revealing nature of God within the first eighteen verses. Why would David do this? Why not add this portion to another Psalm? It just doesn't seem to fit in here. But isn't this the point of the Psalm! As God revealed Himself to David, in the Psalm, as the Omniscient, Omnipresent, and Omnivident God, He also revealed David's true prophetic identity starting in Psalm 139:19. King David's zeal for upholding the name of God was quite evident in this verse.

As I contemplated studying the Psalm in its entirety, I came to understand it in four phases. King David's own prophetic identity comes to light within the revelation of the multi-faceted character of God's true nature. What does David's prophetic identity tell us about him? Well...

1. He was *wired* by God at birth to be a warrior-king.

2. He was *born* at a specific time in history as God's chosen vessel for his generation.

3. He was *anointed* to defeat and subdue the enemy nations' around Israel.

4. He was *appointed* to bring Israel to its dominion rest.

5. He was *destined* to create the blueprints of the Temple as a dwelling place for God to abide among His people in Jerusalem.

6. He *fulfilled* his prophetic mandate!

King David discovered his prophetic identity by getting to know the Omniscient, Omnipresent, and Omnivident God of the universe. So can we!

- Have you discovered your prophetic identity?

- Do you know what you have been called to do, my life's purpose?

- Are you walking out your true life's purpose prescribed in the eternal book of Psalm 139, which speaks about your life's destiny?

This workbook will take you through the three distinct natures of God's greatness, which reveals His omnipotent nature. In this process, you will be able to discover your life's prophetic purpose by understanding how to detect, discern, and decipher a *prophetic algorithm*. The key of unraveling a prophetic algorithm (the way God speaks to you) is to discern and decipher the multi—sensory and multi-dimensional ways of God's prophetic intent for your life and others.

If you are not paying attention to your prophetic algorithms for your life, you can miss out on key revelatory indicators necessary to unveil your true prophetic identity and purpose, which fill us with faith to move toward our prophetic destiny.

Joel

Section #1 | Defining a Prophetic Algorithm

A prophetic algorithm is simply the way God communicates with you individually based on your spiritual settings. God knows the best way you receive information, as well as revelation. There is no one who understands your **spiritual learning modality** than God Himself. God not only knows your natural learning modalities but also the best forms of revelation to reach you.

First, if you would allow me to explain a learning modality. In an educational setting, our learning modalities can consist of one or more of these lists:

1. Visual (spatial) learning,

2. Kinesthetic (physical or hands-on) learning,

3. Aural (auditory) learning,

4. Social (interpersonal) learning,

5. Solitary (intra-personal) learning,

6. Verbal (linguistic) learning, and

7. Logical learning (using logic and structure).[1]

Do you know your own learning modalities and how you learn best?

A learning modality is an educational delivery system applied by teachers to present information to students. The masterful teacher applies several learning modalities to ensure students learn and retain the information given in class. Not all students learn alike; each student has one or more learning modalities of their own to receive, process, and retain the information presented by the teacher. For example, a good teacher will apply several learning modalities in the classroom to assess how individual students best receive and retain the information. Once a teacher understands how a group or a particular student learns best, they will be able to apply the best learning modalities suited for the students or a particular student for greater absorption.

Spiritual Learning Modalities

God does something similar when delivering revelation to you. After all, God knows the best form of revelation to present to you, so you can detect, discern, and decipher prophetic revelation or what I call a prophetic algorithm. Therefore, you possess a **prophetic code language** God uses on a regular basis to speak to you. For example, the most common way I receive revelation is through my **five spiritual senses, vivid dreams, and night visions**.

---

[1] What are the 7 different learning styles and do they work? July 1st, 2021 by Avado Learning. https://www.avadolearning.com/blog/the-7-different-learning-styles-and-what-they-mean/, accessed on 3.12.23

What are your top three revelatory learning modalities that God applies to you to utter a prophetic word?

Go to **Appendix A** to take your assessment to reveal the top three ways you receive prophetic revelation.

Defining a Prophetic Algorithm

The way God communicates with a person is based upon that person's spiritual language. God knows when and how to break into your spirit, heart, soul, and mind and deposit heaven's gems into your life. God knows how to reach you and how to get your attention. David mentions, in Psalm 139, that God is "intimate with all of our ways." And, because God knows you so well, and every rhythm of your life from morning to bedtime is known by Him, God is able to tailor the best way to release divine revelation to fit your life's algorithms.

David, in **Psalm 139:1-6**, reveals your life has an algorithm. This **personal algorithm** is based on your life's patterns, habits, and the behaviors you exhibit on a regular basis each day. God, therefore, is familiar with all your ways.

The way God speaks to you is what I call a **Prophetic Algorithm:**

The word *algorithm* comes from the world of technology, which means *a list of instructions and rules a computer needs to do to complete a task from start to finish.*[2]

---

[2] Algorithm definition, online 2.28.2023

> The Holy Spirit is the software you have been given who will provide you with the prophetic revelation from the initiation phase to finish.

For example, how does an email know how to function? Well, there's an algorithm built into the software that tells the email how to function, from the initiation phase of bringing up an email to the filling in of data and to pushing the send button on your computer so the email goes to its intended recipient.

In a similar way, God has a **prophetic code language** designed especially for you to receive, discern and decipher a prophetic word.

For example, the Spirit of God may give you a dream in the night with a certain narrative with certain characters and symbols. When you wake up, the dream is still heavily impressed upon your mind — this impression of the dream won't leave you until you begin to look into its meaning. God gave you the wisdom so you can be able to discern and to decipher a prophetic algorithm's meaning. Sometimes, the divine communication and interpretation will be simple to decipher; other times, it will take some prayer and meditation to break the prophetic code.

Paul's Spiritual Algorithms

If you are still skeptical about the way God speaks to you individually, then take a look at the Apostle Paul's prophetic code language in the book of Acts. I broke his prophetic code one night during a personal study time when God happened to speak to Paul predominately during the night. The Apostle Paul's night encounters are well noted by Luke, the author of the book of Acts, who states emphatically:

"And **a vision** appeared to Paul **in the night**. A man of Macedonia..." — Acts 16:9

"Now **the Lord** spoke to Paul in the **night by a vision**." — Acts 18:9

"But **the following night the Lord stood by him** (Paul) and said, 'Be of good cheer Paul, for as you have testified about me in Jerusalem, so you must also bear witness at Rome.'" — Acts 23:11

"For **this very night** there stood before me **an angel of the God** to whom I belong and whom I worship, and he said, 'Do not be afraid, Paul...'" — Acts 27:23—24

The apostle Paul's **prophetic code language** included "**night-time visions and visitations**." Paul was inclined to receive revelation at night-time. By all means, this does not dismiss the fact that Paul received revelation during the day-time; he was just more prone to night-time prophetic visions and visitations. However, the four scriptures listed are enough to measure a prophetic algorithmic pattern of revelatory intervention in the book of Acts. You must have the testimony of two or three witnesses to solidify a pattern or a truth... in this case, we have four witnesses.

I have a personal theory about Paul's night encounters:

_____

_____

_____

14

It seems Paul was a **Shamar Watchman**[3] who would "pray and watch" during night hours or in the early morning hours, then standby to hear a prophetic word from the Lord. God would speak to him when he was awake during a night-watch or perhaps received a night visions when he went back to sleep. God knows your prophetic algorithms (Psalm 139:1—6), therefore, He will address you accordingly to your code language or spiritual learning modality.

The word *shamar* means to guard, to keep watch or to be a watchman. It emphasizes the protective element of the prophet's mantle. Shamar can refer to guarding a flock, the heart, the mind, a nation, or a city from outside attack or ungodly influences. It is used in reference to keeping (guarding) the gates or entries to cities. Each local church needs a prophetic guard. This is not just one prophet but a company of prophets who help guard the church from the invasion of the enemy.

Breaking Down the Components of a Prophetic Algorithm

Now, let's apply the definition of an algorithm taken from the technological world to the prophetic ministry. This way, you will have a working definition going forward of what a prophetic algorithm is, which will bring more clarity to your prophetic development throughout this course.

---

[3] Understanding the Role of the Watchman, Charisma, March 21, 2013. https://mycharisma.com/spiritled-living/prayer-devotion/understanding-the-role-of-a-watchman/

The Four Components of a Prophetic Algorithm:

1. **Revelation (Detecting):** A prophetic revelation is a set of instructions, an utterance, given by God through various means. We must learn to detect divine revelation in its various forms when it comes our way.

2. **Rules of Interpretation (Discerning and Deciphering):** There are rules for discerning and deciphering (interpretation) a prophetic algorithm, which are required to bring you to a place of understanding with what God wants to convey to you.

3. **Receiver:** You are like the computer, a human shell with spiritual software, the Holy Spirit, who is the medium God uses to convey a message for yourself, to someone near you, or to a group of people, like in a congregation. The revelation maybe for you or someone else.

4. **Results (Direct Outcome):** Understanding the prophetic revelation is the task God wants you to discern and to decipher for yourself or for someone else. You will know when the algorithm has completed its cycle.

A prophetic algorithm, therefore, is the process of **detecting** a prophecy, then **discerning** its source, and **deciphering** its meaning so you get to the **direct—outcome** of God's prophetic intent.

Now, do you have a basic understanding of what a **prophetic algorithm** is? (Please also go to **Appendix B** to see a full breakdown). If you are still uncertain about it, let's provide you with alternative examples, starting with a bedtime routine.

1. An Algorithm in a Bedtime Routine

Let's simplify the meaning of a prophetic algorithm for the sake of understanding it better and making it more applicable in your life. For example, did you know a bedtime routine has an algorithm all of its own?

— What do you do on a regular basis before you go to bed?

— Can you list the things you do in order each night?

Allow me to list a generic nightly (algorithm) routine, which may differ from person to person. A bedtime routine is a set of activities you perform in the same order every night, in the 30 to 60 minutes before you go to bed. Bedtime routines can vary but often include calming activities like taking a warm bath or shower, reading, journaling, or meditation.[4] You can add other algorithms, such as brushing your teeth, flossing, putting on your pajamas, and perhaps some romance.

Note: Over time you develop a habit, a prescribed pattern, or what is known as an *algorithm.*

2. An Algorithm in a Food Recipe

The recipe for baking a cake, the method we use to change the oil of a car, the process of doing laundry, and the habits we have formed before going to bed are all algorithms.

---

[4] Bedtime Routines for Adults by Danielle Pacheco, Staff Writer and Heather Wright, Psychologist. January 6th 2023.
https://www.sleepfoundation.org/sleep-hygiene/bedtime-routine-for-adultsm

A food recipe has an algorithm all of its own. A food recipe consists of various ingredients, with varied measurements for each ingredient. However, the algorithm starts with the desire of the Chef who decides what to bake or to cook. The Chef then takes the various ingredients and measures them out into a bowl, and mixes them up. Once the proper blend and taste is produced, the oven is heated to its proper temperature. The Chef then sets the time allotted for the dish to cook to specifications.

These are all considered algorithms for a dinner casserole or for the baking of a cake or dessert. Oftentimes, an algorithm continues after baking is complete. If it's a cake, for example, then you apply the icing on top and around the cake and sprinkle it with your own personal delights so it's ready for a visual presentation. The algorithm ends when you take a taste of it—yummy!

Do your best to write out your own working definition of a prophetic algorithm:

I define a **prophetic algorithm** as_____

_____

_____

_____

_____

_____

_____

_____

_____

Jesus Meets Zaccheus:
A Biblical Application of a Prophetic Algorithm

First, let's read Luke 19:1-10, thoroughly before diving into this section of your workbook.

As Jesus traveled the road, large crowds gathered along the path to greet Him. As Jesus came along the path, God, the Father broke His stride to give Him a **prophetic word of knowledge** (a verbal form of a prophetic algorithm), which was a man's name. God, the Father, brought the name of Zaccheus to the forefront of Jesus' mind.

How else would Jesus know a man's name in a strange town among so many strangers?

The most interesting thing in this short narrative was, what was Zaccheus doing at this particular time when Jesus called out to him by his own name?

Zaccheus was short in stature and needed a little lift above the crowd, so he climbed upon a tree limb above all the onlookers. All Zaccheus wanted to do was to capture a glimpse of the Miracle Worker who would soon pass by him. Instead, to Zaccheus' surprise, Jesus looked over in his direction and said:

"Zaccheus, today I must have lunch with you."

This prophetic word of knowledge directed Jesus to focus upon a man hanging from a tree. However, there's *another* prophetic algorithm we tend to miss in this story.

Now, can you discern and decipher what this prophetic algorithm is?

> Prophecy is not just about "hearing" what God is saying, it is also about "seeing" the signs God puts in front of us each day to confirm the prophetic algorithm.

The prophetic algorithm God—the Father had provided to His Son Jesus was the prophetic imagery of a **"tree"** along the path with **"a man hanging upon it."** This prophetic algorithm included both hearing (auditory—a word of knowledge) and visual imagery (visual—seeing a man hanging from a tree).

Now, do you see how a prophetic algorithm works?

I wonder what went through Jesus' mind at this point?

Now, what does the imagery of a "tree" and a "man hanging from it" symbolize to Jesus at this point?

The answer is found in scripture, which is why we need a thorough understanding of the scriptures to be familiar with the teachings from the stories provided therein. You would need some **scripture background to discern and decipher this hidden prophetic algorithm**. The answer is found in Deuteronomy 21:22-23, where the narrative says:

Prophecy is a combination of multi-sensory devices, such as a word of knowledge, a visual image, and even the reputation of a condemned city like Jericho.

"And if a man has committed a crime punishable by death and he is put to death, and **you hang him on a tree**, his body shall not remain all night on the tree, but you shall bury him the same day, **for a hanged man is cursed by God**."

The curse came through Adam, who took and ate the forbidden fruit from the Tree of Knowledge of Good and Evil. We, you and I, have inherited the curse of sin through Adam's disobedience. In reality, we are all guilty of sin, which is **punishable by death "by hanging upon a tree**." We were **all culpable of the crime**, and therefore, we have **all become complicit and guilty of the transgression too**—not just Adam.

In God's eternal wisdom, although we are all deserving of death, Jesus intervened on our behalf to become the "curse" for us. For the apostle Paul says in Galatians 3:13 (NIV):

"Christ redeemed us from the curse of the law by becoming a curse for us, for it is written: 'Cursed is everyone who is hung on a pole [or tree].'"

If you are not familiar with the scriptures, you can miss a valuable insight embedded in the story, which God placed before your very eyes to **discern and decipher a prophetic algorithm**. Eating a meal was not the only objective at the lunch table — salvation would become the central topic. To **discern and decipher a prophetic**

algorithm, one must be spiritually aware of the things before us so we can see what God is doing. So, make sure you look deeper into the text to derive meaning from its images, and historical settings, etc.?

_____

_____

_____

_____

_____

_____

_____

_____

_____

_____

_____

_____

_____

_____

_____

_____

A Review of Zaccheus' Prophetic Algorithm

Hearing What God is Saying: The **first prophetic algorithm**, a word of knowledge, occurred when Jesus encountered Zaccheus along His path. Jesus called Zaccheus by his first name. How did Jesus know his name? It was a "word of knowledge" given to him by His Father.

Seeing What God is Doing: The **second prophetic algorithm** is somewhat hidden, but if you look closer, you can see it. The total image before Jesus consisted of a tree, and a sinner just happened to be hanging upon it. Jesus, at this point, was reminded of His mission to redeem the lost, of which Zaccheus symbolized the curse for the time being.

The **third and final prophetic algorithm** is the setting where this story takes place. It happened to be the city of Jericho. Jericho was the first city the children of Israel invaded and captured within the Promised Land. The entire city would be considered as a first-fruits offering unto God, meaning everything in it, including the treasure, was to be totally dedicated to God alone. No one else could take this honor upon themselves — the city and everything in it belonged to God alone.

Israel came under a curse because one individual named Achan held back some of the idols for himself and hid them in his tent. Therefore, the children of Israel came under God's judgement. The culprit was soon identified and dealt with. God would not allow sin to permeate the holy community upon its historical arrival into the Promised Land.

Joshua pronounced a curse upon the city, and it remained uninhabited for a long time.

The city of Jericho had been occupied for sometime by the time Jesus passed through it and encountered Zaccheus. Jericho may have had prophetic significance due to the curse placed upon it by Joshua. Jesus, the restorer of the breach, redeemed the reputation of the city by redeeming one sinner named Zaccheus.

> If you can detect a prophetic algorithm in scripture, then you will be able to detect one in your own life.

Logos and Rhema

Now you should know the value of knowing God through His written word (Logos), and hearing an utterance (Rhema) from His loving voice through His Spirit. The story of Zaccheus should alert you to be passionate for Him in profusely reading the scriptures, praying, meditating upon His word, and then waiting in quietness to see the various forms that God speaks.

Jesus was given a name through a prophetic word (Rhema: an utterance at the moment). Then He saw a man "hanging on a tree" (Logos: the written word of God, the scriptures). Jesus was then exposed to the book of Deuteronomy and the meaning of the reputation of that city. Therefore, a man hanging from a tree meant "he who hung on a tree" was cursed. Jesus then asked a sinner, a man condemned to eternal death, out to lunch, and the rest was history. God guided Jesus to His intended target. This is called *prophetic navigation.*

Now, take a look at Diagram A to visualize the fullness of the previous prophetic algorithm.

Diagram A:
Zaccheus' Prophetic Algorithm

Jesus was traveling through the City of Jericho

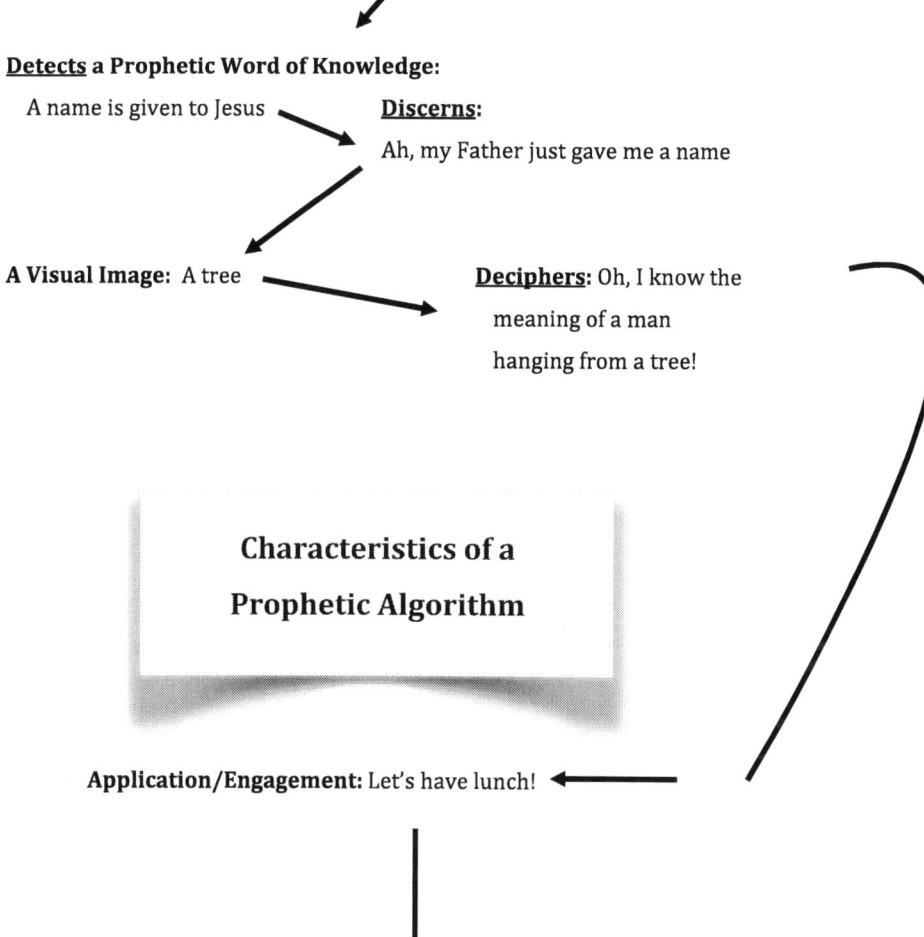

Detects a Prophetic Word of Knowledge:

A name is given to Jesus

Discerns:

Ah, my Father just gave me a name

A Visual Image: A tree

Deciphers: Oh, I know the meaning of a man hanging from a tree!

Characteristics of a Prophetic Algorithm

Application/Engagement: Let's have lunch!

The Direct Outcome of this Prophetic Algorithm:

Zaccheus shares his testimony, and Jesus affirms his Salvation.

Class Exercise: The Macedonian Call

Based upon the information and revelation you received from reading **Acts 16:6-10 (NIV)**, or what is often referred to as the Macedonian Call, configure your own algorithm on the next page, much like **Diagram A:**

6

Paul and his companions traveled throughout the region of Phrygia and Galatia, having been kept by the Holy Spirit from preaching the word in the province of Asia.

7

When they came to the border of Mysia, they tried to enter Bithynia, but the Spirit of Jesus would not allow them to.

8

So they passed by Mysia and went down to Troas.

9

During the night, Paul had a vision of a man of Macedonia standing and begging him, "Come over to Macedonia and help us."

10

After Paul had seen the vision, we got ready at once to leave for Macedonia, concluding that God had called us to preach the gospel to them.

Now, on the next page, you will fill in your own algorithm based on the information in the scripture passage just mentioned.

Fill in the Prophetic Algorithm of the Macedonian Call (Refer to Diagram A)

What are the multi-sensory applications (**detecting**) being used in this prophetic algorithm?

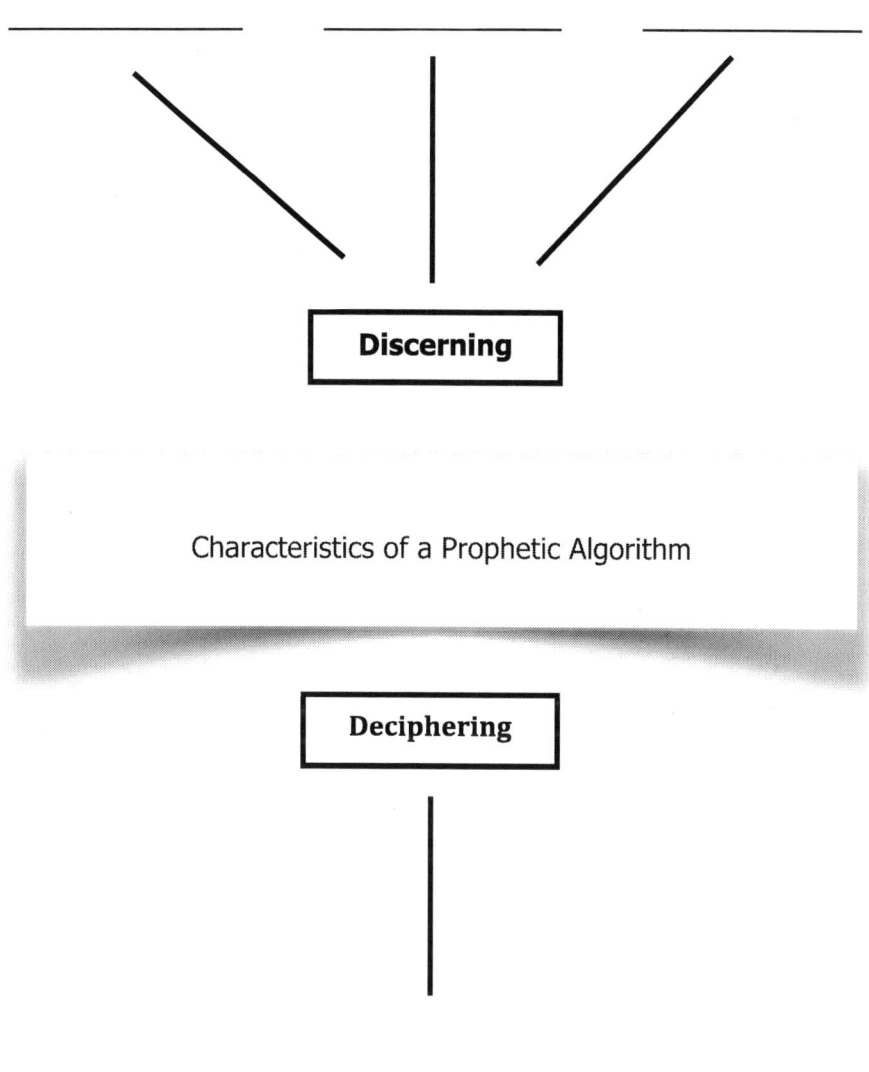

_____   _____   _____

Discerning

Characteristics of a Prophetic Algorithm

Deciphering

_____

What is the direct outcome?

Group Questionnaire:

What is happening with the apostolic team under Paul's supervision?

Who is on this team? If you are familiar with who they were, then what are their names and gifts on this list?

_____   _____

_____   _____

_____   _____

_____   _____

There seems to be more than one person on the team receiving revelation for the direction of the group (the algorithm).

_____

_____

_____

_____

Is spiritual warfare oftentimes associated with the prophetic ministry? If so, why?

_____

_____

_____

_____

Diagram B:
The Components of a Prophetic Algorithm

Detecting a Multi-sensory & Multi-Dimensional

Prophetic Algorithm from God

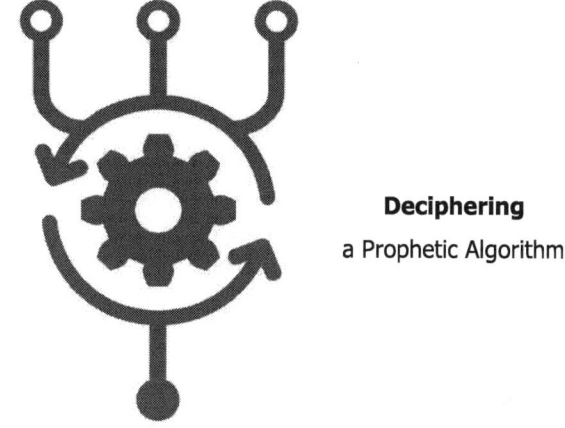

Discerning

a Prophetic Algorithm

Deciphering

a Prophetic Algorithm

The **Direct Outcome** of the Prophetic Algorithm

Notes

Section #2	# God's Multi-faceted Nature: God is Omniscient: All-Knowing

The Multi-faceted Nature of God

David is the author of Psalm 139. This psalm has a degree of familiarity upon it, meaning the psalm has become all too familiar in our casual reading of it. Therefore, we are not able to squeeze out a deeper revelation from the text as we should. The key to understanding Psalm 139 is to step back in order to dive deeper into what David was attempting to convey to us. Then, we can break down the psalm into smaller parts.

> When approaching a biblical text, we first need to look at the map of the forest, before journeying into the various paths of a hike.

As I was preparing for a prophetic workshop for a conference in Las Vegas in January of 2023, I was led to read and study Psalm 139. As I read and meditated upon it over and over for about a month, the Spirit unlocked some unique gems to me that I had not seen before. I will categorize the psalm for you into four parts. As I looked through the forest of the whole Psalm, I saw four hiking trails emerge. These four hiking trails are:

1. Psalm 139:1-6: God is Omniscient — God is all-knowing.

2. Psalm 139:7-10: God is Omnipresent — God is present in all places at one time.

3. Psalm 139:11-18: God is Omnivident — God is all-seeing.

4. Psalm 139:19-24: David's Prophetic Identity — David was wired to be a warrior-king.

In the following sections, I will take you through each section so you can experience how David experienced and interacted with God in a revelatory encounter to finally arrive at the revelation and confirmation of his prophetic identity.

God is Omniscient: Psalm 139:1-6

First and foremost, God is omniscient, meaning that He knows all things. The writer of the book of Hebrews notes something similar:

"Nothing in all creation is hidden from God's sight. Everything is uncovered and laid bare before the eyes of him to whom we must give account."[5]

---

[5] Hebrews 4:13 NIV

Can you fathom God's greatness at this point? Even David, in verse six, was blown away by this magnificent revelation:

"Such knowledge is too wonderful for me, too lofty for me to attain."[6]

David was beside himself to understand this prophetic insight of God's perfect awareness of each person in the world at one time! According to the **World-O-Meter**, at the time of the writing of this section of this workbook on 3.14.23, the world's population stood at an astounding **8,021,900,000**.[7] This population on the World-O-Meter is rapidly increasing day by day and every single second of the day of each week.

> "God counts the number of the stars; He calls them all by name. Great is our Lord, and mighty in power; His understanding is infinite." — Psalm 147:4 & 5

If you Google World-O-Meter, what would the population be right now? Write the number below:

The current World-O-Meter is currently at: _____

on _____ (Month) _____(Day) and _____ (Year).

Calculation:

Current Meter:_____,_____, _____,000

Minus My Meter: 8,021,900,000 rounded figure on 3.14.2023

---

[6] Psalm 139:6
[7] World Population Clock: https://www.worldometers.info/world-population/, accessed on 1.27.2023

The difference now is:_____, _____, _____, _____ This is how much the population has grown since I first researched this factoid.

By doing this exercise, I want you to see God's capacity with an infinite and limitless knowledge of each individual on the planet at this very moment in time!

Can you imagine? At this very moment, God knows every intimate detail about every single living person on the face of the earth! This knowledge is too lofty for me to attain too! I'm simply blown away by it! What an amazing God we serve!

God Knows Your Life's Algorithms

Let's see how God knows every single detail about your life. Let's start by breaking down Psalm 139 into its basic parts according to the outline previously given. Take a few moments now to read and meditate on the first section of Psalm 139:1-6, which reveals **God's omniscience**:

1

You have searched me, Lord, and you know me.

2

You know when I sit and when I rise; you perceive my thoughts from afar.

3

You discern my going out and my lying down; you are familiar with all my ways.

4

Before a word is on my tongue you, Lord, know it completely.

5

You hem me in behind and before, and you lay your hand upon me.

35

Such knowledge is too wonderful for me, too lofty for me to attain.

When King David wrote down the revelation of this Psalm, he was beside himself on how God could know him so well and still be able to love him unconditionally. This knowledge went beyond David's comprehension — he didn't know what to do with it! As I have stated before — this revelation simply blew his mind!

God Knows Our Daily Algorithms

In the first six verses of this Psalm, David provides us a glimpse into God's omniscient nature. God knows every part of **our daily routine,** from the time we wake up in the morning until we lay down again at night and everything in between. God even knows our very first thought in the morning before it even forms in our mind and rolls out of our tongue. He knows our **morning rituals, patterns,** and even down to our **motivations.** He is familiar with our **pace and stride,** meaning our energy levels at every speed, whether slow, steady, or energetic.

God is with us throughout the day as we walk along our daily path. Therefore, He knows the **paths** we are going to take before we take them on our daily commute and any last-minute **alternative routes** before we even consider them. This is God's **omniscient knowledge of our life's daily algorithms.**

What does your morning routine look like each day? List five things you normally do when you wake up? Do this for several days to see your own pattern.

1. _____

_____

_____

_____

2. _____

_____

_____

_____

3. _____

_____

_____

_____

4. _____

_____

_____

_____

5. _____

_____

_____

_____

Prophecy is Multi-Sensory in Nature

Prophecy is multi-sensory in nature. What I mean is prophecy, oftentimes, stimulates us in a multi-sensory fashion, such as **vivid dreams, visions, and impressions, through our spiritual senses, night visions, etc**. In addition, like the story you are about to be exposed too, prophecy is reinforced through **patterns, repetitions, and sequences**. Prophecy can come to us in the form of a wave or a sequence of waves, one right after another. For example, it resembles the waves of the sea breaching upon the sandy shoreline, one right after the other, with a gentle or ferocious force in an algorithmic fashion. God's voice can be gentle or ferocious in nature.

For example, we get a piece of revelation at one moment, then another form of revelation comes in a different form, and perhaps a third wave of revelation will brush over us just to make sure we hear God's voice clearly. God does this to ensure we hear and receive the desires of His heart and mind for ourselves and for others.

Does this sequence of prophecy remind you of anyone in the Bible?

The Prophetic Algorithm for Peter at the Tanner's House

My previous illustration about the waves brushing upon the shoreline should have brought Peter to the forefront of your mind. In a trance, God was preparing Peter, who was momentarily staying at the Tanner's house by the sea, to go and meet a Gentile man in his home. As Peter was resting briefly at the Tanner's house, he was easing into an afternoon nap on the rooftop, awaiting his lunch meal. As Peter started to drift into his nap, he was soon stimulated by a sequence of visual waves splashing upon him. Then, all of a sudden, Peter received a **culinary vision in multi-sensory form in three repetitive patterns**.

The receptive layers were visual in nature with four-footed animals, a menu unlawful for Jews to consume based on the Mosaic law. God was testing Peter's **religious palette** with a non-kosher food menu. Peter immediately resisted the idea at first until **the third wave** brushed upon him. Luke, the narrator, notes:

> "While Peter was still thinking about the vision, the Spirit said to him, 'Three men are at the door are looking for you. So get up and go downstairs. Do not hesitate to go with them, for I have sent them.'"

While Peter was attempting to interpret (**discern and decipher**) the vision, the Holy Spirit spoke to him, thus adding another layer (or algorithm) to the prophecy. God has many ways to convey His prophetic desires.

Remember, prophecy is multi-sensory in nature.

God speaks through a variation of prophetic receptors (Prophecy is multi-sensory in nature) to transfer the desires of His heart into our hearts. One way God speaks is through our spiritual eye-gate; another is through the spiritual auditory sense of hearing, the olfactory sense of smell, our spiritual palette, and even touch or feeling, which is most commonly known as a prophetic impression.

> Some prophetic impressions highlight a part of your own body to identify the area of healing needed in another person's body.

What other layers of prophecy do you see, if any, in this prophetic encounter with Peter in Acts 10? Write out your thoughts here:

_____

_____

_____

_____

_____

_____

_____

_____

_____

Prophecy is Multi-dimensional in Nature

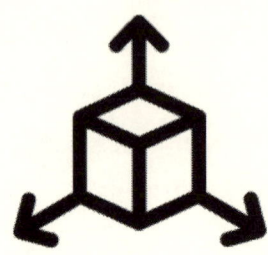

What do I mean by "prophecy" is multi-dimensional in nature? I mean two things. First, we inhabit a **natural dimension**; therefore, God uses symbols and images we are familiar with to convey a message to us. Second, we also experience a **supernatural dimension**. We are spirit beings incased in a body. We are creatures made with **flesh and bone** but with an added feature: the **Holy Spirit** resides within us. **Prophecy encompasses both a physical and a supernatural dimension.** God works through familiar symbols, such as the food presented to Peter in the previous story, but with a spiritual interpretation and application. In this prophecy, God was attempting to break down the barriers of division which existed between the Jews and the Gentiles. It was time to bind them together into one spiritual family.

> Prophecy encompasses both a physical and a supernatural dimension. God works through familiar symbols, such as the food presented to Peter in the previous story, but with a spiritual interpretation.

God understands the world we inhabit, so He is able to connect us to the supernatural world by using **common symbols** you and I have come to understand through our past experiences. For example, Jesus told His disciples, "You are the light of the world." Jesus was using a natural symbol to explain the supernatural power we possess as believers to expose the hidden agenda (occult) and the schemes (strategies) of our common archenemy — the Devil.

On a side note, I remember when a visiting evangelist asked me to pray for him. When I closed my eyes to pray, I saw the backside of a penny. It was the Lincoln Memorial. When I told him what I saw — his eyes got really big. He then told me he was asked to preach in an "open-air" meeting at the steps of the Lincoln Memorial in Washington, D.C., the very thing he was secretly asking us to pray for him. **The penny had a natural side to it, with a spiritual application**. This is what we mean by prophecy being "multi-dimensional" in nature.

When Peter received the vision of the four-footed animals upon a bed sheet flowing in the wind, God was attempting to literally break an existing religious paradigm he had developed as a Jew. God was now challenging a long-held belief and practice about the dietary laws found in the Law of Moses by connecting it to a menu of which the Gentiles delighted in. God was opening a window into the supernatural world by using a common symbol of his diet, a food provision in the Law, restricting the Jewish people from certain foods. God was challenging Peter's long-held beliefs about a religious menu.

Prophecy is multi-dimensional in nature — it presents itself supernaturally, oftentimes using common symbols and experiences we are familiar with in the natural realm so we can better decipher a prophetic algorithm.

God revealed His heart to Peter only to disrupt and dismantle his hidden prejudices as to shift him into a new wineskin — a new structure. Peter wasn't a prophet per-se, as in the pure office of a prophet, but we are all prophetic at some level. Prophecy is not just for prophets alone. Many others in the church body can hear God's voice and express it in their own way.

_____

_____

_____

_____

_____

_____

_____

_____

_____

_____

_____

The Multi-dimensional Nature of Prophecy:
Prophecy Can Be Delivered in Many Forms

Can you think of ways of how a prophetic word can be delivered to a person or group? I have listed several ways I have seen a prophetic word delivered during my tenure in the prophetic ministry. Let's examine a few:

1. *Prophetic Acts*: A prophetic act is voiceless in nature, it is delivered through skits, dramas, or actions of a person. Refer to Ezekiel 4.

2. *Prophetic Evangelism*: A prophetic word of knowledge is given, and a person feels moved or drawn to give their life to Christ. Refer to John 4.

3. *Prophetic Confirmation*: This is where God provides you a confirmation of something He has already spoken over your life. Refer to Luke 24:14-35.

4. *Prophetic Conversations*: People will pick up the heart of God in a normal conversations, much like the Road to Emmaus story. Refer to Luke 24:14-35.

5. *Prophetic Preaching*: An anointed sermon can speak to different people in different ways, where God is able to convey His heart and mind to the multitudes. Referring to Acts 2, Peter's sermon was prophetic preaching.

6. *Prophetic Songs*: We see David prophesying in songs throughout the psalms in various forms. Refer to the Psalms.

7. *Prophetic Words of Knowledge*: When God gives a prophetic person detailed information about someone, only to shift that person's belief to God. Refer to John 4, the woman at the well.

Can you think of other types of prophecy being presented in a multi-dimensional way?

_____

_____

_____

_____

_____

_____

_____

_____

_____

_____

_____

_____

_____

_____

Section #3 | Prophetic Algorithms: Deciphering Patterns, Repetitions, and Sequences

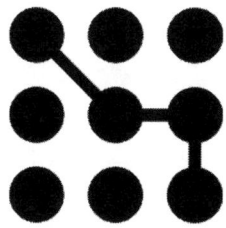

Prophetic algorithms are sometimes released in patterns, repetitions and sequences. Sometimes, God uses one of these or a combination of them at one time. The apostle Peter experienced all three at one time. Let's examine a prophetic encounter to see how this prophetic encounter worked out for Peter.

Peter, for example, was branded with the number three throughout Jesus' ministry. The number three (3) was part of his prophetic algorithm (**Prophetic Code Language**) throughout his entire life. It started when Jesus added Peter, James, and John into His inner circle — a core group of **three disciples**. These three disciples were present with Jesus at critical times in His ministry. One of these critical moments occurred when Jesus secluded Himself and His inner circle to a mountain.

> A Prophetic Algorithm is the unique way God connects to you, and within time, you develop a prophetic code language of your own.

At this mountain, something very interesting happened, two men appeared in dazzling light and white clothing. They just happened to be Moses—the law giver, and Elijah—the prophet, respectively. Peter, being the more vocal of the three, said he would erect temporary shelters to house all three of them; Jesus, Moses, and Elijah. Then, a glory cloud enveloped them. Then a voice came from the majestic cloud affirming, "This is My Son, I am well pleased with Him." What an experience to behold? I am convinced this incident was branded in all three of these disciples' memories for the rest of their lives.

On another occasion, Jesus prophesied to Peter, saying he would deny Him **three times** before the rooster crowed. When it happened, around 3 am in the morning, just like Jesus said it would, Peter was beside Himself and went into an emotional tailspin filled with guilt and shame for a period of time.

Then, during the post-resurrection appearances, this next incident was the **third time** (take note: another number 3) Jesus had appeared to them. At this point, Jesus took the time to restore Peter with three similar statements, starting in verse 14:[8]

---

[8] John 21:14-17

14

This was now the third time Jesus appeared to his disciples after he was raised from the dead.

15

When they had finished eating, Jesus said to Simon Peter, "Simon son of John, do you love me more than these?"
"Yes, Lord," he said, "you know that I love you."
Jesus said, "Feed my lambs."

16

Again Jesus said, "Simon son of John, do you love me?"
He answered, "Yes, Lord, you know that I love you."
Jesus said, "Take care of my sheep."

17

The third time he said to him,
"Simon son of John, do you love me?"
Peter was hurt because Jesus asked him the third time, "Do you love me?"
He said, "Lord, you know all things; you know that I love you."
Jesus said, "Feed my sheep."

— Do you see a pattern developing in Peter's life during this sequence of questioning?

— Do you know what it was?

This is the essence of a Prophetic Algorithm.
Your history with God can reveal certain algorithms for your life
for a particular encounter.

First, this was the **third time** Jesus had appeared to the disciples. Second, during the meal, Jesus engaged Peter in a sequence of questioning by repeating the same question **three times**. Jesus wanted to restore Peter and shift his confidence from a deep pit of despair and shame to active status once again. Ah, yes, **Peter was branded with the number three.** Whenever the number three came upon Peter's lifeline, he knew God was attempting to speak to him.

Peter's 3-fold Vision, the 3 Visitors, and a 3 Day Journey

Peter's vision on the rooftop of the Tanner's house by the sea has to be the best example of a prophetic algorithm. This prophetic encounter has all three **patterns, repetitions, and sequences** attached to it.

This **trance possessed a multi-dimensional** and **multi-sensory prophetic nature**. First, as Peter is on the rooftop resting while

49

awaiting for his lunch, the narrative notes he was hungry and fell asleep. While he is in between the state of sleep and cognitive perception, he sees a trance (**visual imagery in a vision**) appear before his eyes.

A trance is a sleep-like altered state of consciousness usually characterized by partly suspended animation with diminished or absent sensory and motor activity, a spiritual state of profound abstraction or absorption.[9]

In a trance, Peter sees a sheet fall from heaven with four-footed animals upon it, and a voice appeals to his **auditory senses,** saying, "Peter, kill and eat." Peter then responds, 'By no means, I have never eaten anything unclean'" (**the sense of taste**). Three of the five spiritual senses were tapped in this prophetic algorithm. The **trance** repeats itself **three** times, and then it disappears. Take note: a **pattern** is present; the sheet with the four-footed animals is **repeated** three times. So far, we have a **repetitive pattern** and the **first sequence of three** events.

Peter then awakens and gains his full senses. As he is contemplating the meaning of the dream, all of a sudden, **three men (the second sequence begins**) are standing at the door of the Tanner's house asking for Peter. How did he know this information? The **Holy Spirit** prompted Peter and told him the second part of a **sequence** of events with the **number three** present.

Peter is familiar with the number three at this point (Remember: Peter denied Jesus three times, and Jesus attempted to restore Peter

---

[9] Trance: Merriam Webster Online; https://www.merriam-webster.com/dictionary/trance

three times, etc.). So Peter is familiar with the pattern of "threes." At this time, he is really wondering what God is up to because it was late into the night. Peter boards the three visitors for the night (On Day 1 - **the third sequence begins**) at the Tanner's House. The next day (Day 2), they travel to Caesarea. They stay the night at a boarding house, and then, on the following day (on Day 3) they arrive to their destination.

There are three incidents that fulfill a **sequence of three events,** and with these three instances, you see the number three in each one.

Do you see what I see here?

Refer to **Diagram C: Patterns, Repetitions, and Sequences** on the next page for a visual representation of the dream and recurrence of 3's in each sequence.

Diagram C:
Prophetic Patterns, Repetitions & Sequences

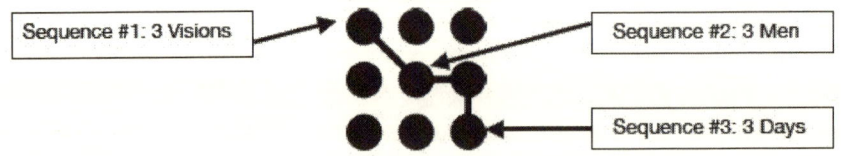

When Peter arrived at Cornelius's home, he realized something very important. Peter stated to the Gentiles present, saying:

> "You are well aware that it is against our law for a Jew to associate with or visit a Gentile. But God has shown me that I should not call anyone impure or unclean. So when I was sent for, I came without raising any objection. May I ask why you sent for me?"

The response from Cornelius is quite interesting in itself. I call this a **prophetic confirmation**:

> "Three days ago, I was in my house praying at this hour, at three in the afternoon..."

How many times does the number "three" show up in this sentence? As Peter was listening to Cornelius' testimony, it was riddled with a sequence of the number three. By this time, Peter knew he was in the right place and doing the right thing in the eyes of God.

The prophetic algorithm has now completed its task, from **detecting** to **discerning** and **deciphering** it properly, (**Go to Appendix B now for a visual diagram**).

Peter followed through on the prophetic utterance given to him, which brought him to his objective; to visit and meet with the Gentile named Cornelius. When this event occurred, God then poured out the Holy Spirit upon the Gentiles, much like the pattern seen during the first Pentecost in Acts 2, as they gathered in the Upper Room. The prophetic algorithm has done its job; the prophetic word is fulfilled.

Do you now understand what a prophetic algorithm is?

Now take a look at the visual chart of a prophetic algorithm in **Diagram D**, and refer to **Appendix B** at the rear of this workbook.

Diagram D:
Peter's Prophetic Algorithm

1. <u>Detecting</u> a   Prophetic Algorithm

Trance ——————————▶ **Three Times**

(Vision—A Repetitious Pattern)   (End of Sequence #1)

The Revelation is visual, auditory and hits his palette.

While Peter is <u>discerning</u> the Vision

The Holy Spirit speaks ————▶ **Three Men are at the Door**

(Auditory Voice)   (Pattern—Sequence #2)

The Vision is now Unfolding: 2. <u>Discerning and Deciphering</u>

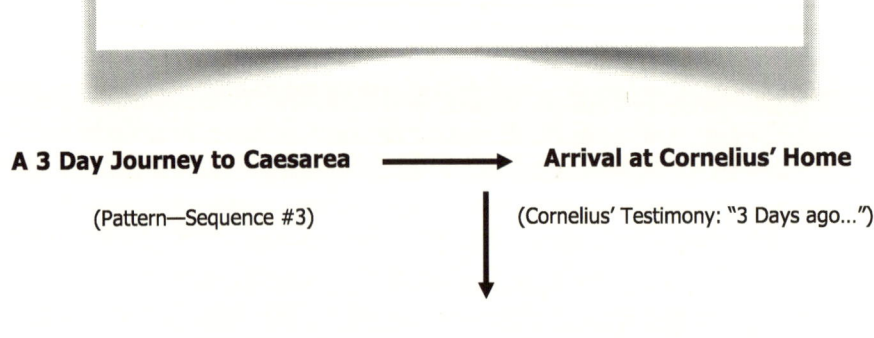

Characteristics of a
Prophetic Algorithm

A 3 Day Journey to Caesarea ————▶ **Arrival at Cornelius' Home**

(Pattern—Sequence #3)   (Cornelius' Testimony: "3 Days ago...")

3. The <u>Direct Outcome</u> of the Prophetic Algorithm:

The Holy Spirit Descends Upon the Gentiles

Notes:

_____

_____

_____

_____

_____

_____

_____

_____

_____

_____

_____

_____

_____

_____

_____

_____

_____

_____

_____

_____

_____

Section #4	God's Multi-faceted Nature: God is Omnipresent — Present Everywhere

God is Omnipresent: Psalm 139: 7-10

God is omnipresent, meaning God's presence can be found anywhere, at any given time. God is available to you 24–7, in all 24 time zones in the natural calendar day cycle. King David asked the following rhetorical questions as he considered the profundity of God's nature in His life. Let's read verses seven through ten:

7

Where can I go from your Spirit? Where can I flee from your presence?

8

If I go up to the heavens, you are there; if I make my bed in the depths, you are there.

9

If I rise on the wings of the dawn if I settle on the far side of the

sea,

10

even there your hand will guide me, your right hand will hold me

fast.

Because God is omnipresent — there is really nowhere you can flee nor hide from His presence! God is everywhere at any given time! You can have access to Him at any given time of the Day, and He has access to you. David then goes on to provide a few examples, one is vertical, and the other is horizontal in nature. On a vertical note, David says, "If I go to the heavens you are there." Of course, the heavens are His handiwork where His throne abides. "If I make my bed in the depths, you are there," too! God abides in the palatial structure in the heavens but can also be found in a tunnel far into the earth's core, even in Sheol.

From a horizontal perspective, David notes, "If I rise on the wings of the dawn; if I settle on the far sides of the sea, you are there to guide me..." David's reference to the "wings of the dawn" is when the Earth spins on its axis, various regions receive light or darkness [10] depending on the rotation of the earth at the time. The wings of the dawn are the fine line between day-light and the line of the dawn. David goes on to say, "If I go to the far seas..." referring to an indication of travel to uncharted territory. Even there, in the yet

---

[10] World Atlas: How Many Time Zones Does the World Have?
https://www.worldatlas.com/articles/how-many-time-zones-does-the-world-have.html

undiscovered areas of the earth, you can find God awaiting your arrival. Even in the far seas, God will meet us there to guide us along our path. **King David was referring to God's presence in time and space.**

Can you imagine, by plane or by sea, in the distance skies above and the extended seas on all sides, you can find God awaiting your arrival in time? God is not distant by any means. He is closer than you can think or can imagine. He is just a cry away from His children, ready to act and to speak life into you.

_____

_____

_____

_____

_____

_____

_____

_____

_____

_____

_____

_____

How Prophecy Works in Time

God eclipses time because of His eternal nature. There are distinct instances in the Bible where God eclipsed time. God can cut into time to reorder things and direct our lives. The following four illustrations are examples of how God intervened in time to move His agenda forward upon humanity:

1. God Pauses Time

The first incident of God eclipsing time is found in Joshua's day. Joshua was fighting a confederation of five kings when, all of a sudden, he encountered a moment in time when he needed additional daylight to defeat his foes. During a long day of battle, as the day was fading into dusk, they were making great advances against their enemy. However, they required more time in the day to continue the fight and to defeat the enemy. So Joshua asked God for the "sun to stand still." It was an unusual request, to say the least. In other words, he was asking God to "pause time" until the Israelites could advance and defeat their formidable foes.

Then, all of a sudden, time stopped, but not their movement in time, as they continued fighting the battle while the "sun stood still" in its place. It wasn't the sun that stood still; it was the earth, which stopped rotating on its axis, keeping the sun at the same angle for quite some time. In other words, they experienced a bit of eternity with no clock ticking away. God had paused time long enough for Israel to destroy their enemy.

2. God Resets Time

In King Hezekiah's day, the prophet Isaiah told the king to prepare himself for the inevitable—he was going to die. However, the king asked Isaiah the prophet for more time and pleaded to God with tearful prayers to extend his life a bit longer. God listened to his request and obliged. The King was granted his wish but asked the prophet for a prophetic sign to know for certain his request would come to pass. The sign from God would show the shadow of the sun dial would be turned back 10 degrees. It is estimated that the time on the sound dial went back to 40 minutes. This was a visible sign notifying Hezekiah of his healing and the extension of his life for many more years to come. So when the sun dial turned back 10 degrees in time, King Hezekiah knew God had answered his prayer. For God all things are possible because He is the creator of time.

3. God Bypasses Time

In the book of Acts (8:39—40), for example, Philip "time-traveled" from one place to another, to a city known as Azotus. This town was 30 km away from his current location. A 30 km walk is estimated to be 18.64 miles. A rigorous yet steady walk on foot would take someone about 4 hours to complete, but Philip was immediately translated to the town of Azotus in a single moment of time. God did this because, in His timing, He had other plans for Philip in another location. God bypassed time by accelerating Philip into his future.

These examples show how God is capable of dealing with time, space, and matter. We tend to forget God abides outside our time continuum. So God is capable of prophesying over your life, and knowing the prophetic word will come to pass at an appointed time.

— Do you believe in "time-travel"?

Now, let's examine why prophecy sometimes takes time to manifest.

4. God Redeems the Time

In Esther's day, an evil decree was set into law on a certain day when the Jews were scheduled for total annihilation. They became powerless and hopeless. This decree was influenced by Haman, who influenced the king to sign the decree into law. Satan, at times, sets a person over those in government to control the laws and redefine the time (Acts 13:6-12). God, however, had set Esther in place because in His foreknowledge, He can see what is coming ahead. So He appoints certain people to be born in time, and positions them to be at the right place in time to expose the fraud.

God used Mordecai to guide Queen Esther to do something about this since she had the ear of the king. When Mordecai addressed Esther, he added a famous line, "Yet who knows whether you have come to the kingdom for such a time as this?"[11] After a time of fasting and prayer, Esther developed a strategy to enter the king's presence. When everything worked out in her favor, the king was able to see the "fraud" perpetrated against the Jews and made another decree to counter the first one. God redeemed the time, by giving the Jews enough time to prepare and to fight against their enemies. What

---

[11] Esther 4:14 NKJV

seemed lost, God was able to redeem the time for the Jews to defeat their enemies.

Prophecy is fulfilled when you are ready to steward your prophetic word!

Abraham's Journey:
A Promise, a Contradiction of Reality, and an Unwavering Faith

Abraham's journey, along with the promises spoken over his life, is a perfect example of **stewarding the prophetic word**. First, God spoke to Abraham because He wanted to create a whole new race through him. At the time, Abraham and Sarai were not capable of bearing children in their old age. Abraham was just 75 when he received the promise. When Abraham became 100 years of age, Issac, the prophetic promise of his life, was born. This span of time consisted of a twenty-five-year gap between the prophetic promise spoken over their lives until its fulfillment.

This is one of the most powerful stories of redemption in the Bible. God restored the child bearing years to them by rearranging time and space for them. The latter years of their life were more glorious than their former years together. The process of the journey they endured to receive what they had hoped for was the key to receiving the prophetic promise. Abraham was considered righteous for his faithfulness throughout all this.

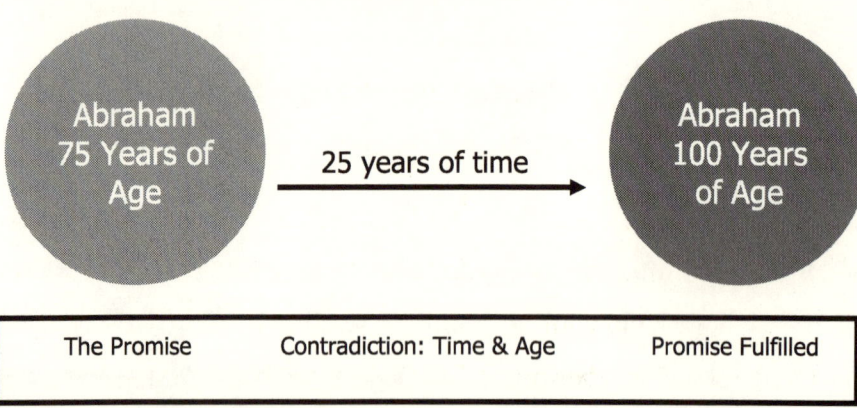

| The Promise | Contradiction: Time & Age | Promise Fulfilled |

In Ecclesiastes 3:11, it notes, "He has made everything beautiful in its time." This alone is an awesome prophetic promise to grab hold of and never let go. We tend to forget Abraham and Sarah were already past their prime time to conceive and have a family when all this happened to them. But, **a prophetic promise from God can change your existing reality,** like it did theirs. God was asking Abraham to believe something that was humanely impossible for anyone to grasp. At his age, every single day, the promise was getting further and further away from being actualized. Can you imagine Abraham's reality with the promise given by God was becoming harder and harder to believe as the years went by, but he kept his faith intact until the promise was actualized. Abraham's faith in God's promises provides us a key to redeeming our body through time; past, present, and future.

> Faith is essential when "time and age" are contradicting your promise.

A Prophetic Word to Plant a Church & Its Fulfillment

At a Women's Conference sometime in 1999, my wife Robyn received two prophetic words from the late Prophetess Cathy Lechner, which were captured on a recording device. The first prophetic word from Cathy was, "You and your husband will minister in the South, but you would not board up your home." I interpreted the prophecy to mean, "We were not moving away from Las Vegas," and "We would not need to rent out our home." Then she went on to say, "You will go and plant a church in the South for about one year, raise up the right leadership team, and then install them as the lead pastors." It was a strange prophetic word for us since, at the time, we did not feel a call out from our current church.

A short time later, the Lead Pastor received a vision to start church extensions or satellite churches within the city of Las Vegas. This next church just so happened to be the third one in line with the five churches from the vision he had received. It just so happened the church purchased an old day care building in the *South* part of town. So, the pastoral team started to pray and strategize as to who would get the nod to plant and lead it.

Diagram F:
If God Said it — It's a Done Deal!

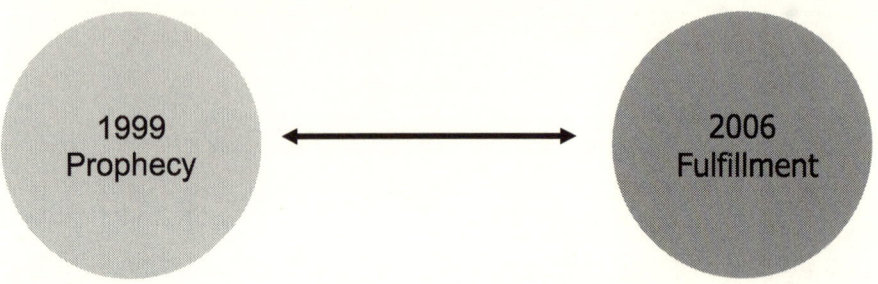

1999 Prophecy ⟷ 2006 Fulfillment

In 2005, a six years apart from the prophetic word, I attended a meeting with the lead pastor and the senior leadership team on the newly purchased property. We sat there praying and discussing which staff member would lead it. After the prayer and some discussion, I then reminded the staff of the prophet's word given by the late Prophet Cathy Lechner concerning my wife and me — that we would go to the "south" for one year and raise up a ministry team and then hand it off. After much consideration, my wife and I were eventually chosen to lead the planting of this new extension. So, for one year, we started to raise up a wonderful team of committed people. The prophetic word over my wife and I was coming to fruition exactly the way the prophetess had told us it would happen.

A Prophetic Confirmation

We had one year to prepare our team for the launch of this extension; it was now 2006. In preparation for our grand opening, we had a neighborhood pancake outreach with bounce houses to attract the neighborhood kids and their parents. We also put together food boxes to give away at an estimated retail cost of $60 per box from donations from local grocery stores. At the end of our outreach, we had some food boxes left over, so we decided to go door—to—door until we gave away all the food boxes.

On our initial route, the driver decided to venture to the left, to a house with the first visible sign of life, where a man was present working in his garage. So we stopped by to give him a box of food and introduce ourselves to our neighbors. My assistant at the time was Frank Holland (Now the Lead Pastor), who walked over to greet the man and to hand him a large food box. After Frank handed the man the food box, he asked the gentleman for his name. The man replied, "My name is Joel Garcia." Overcome by surprise (I could actually see it on his face), Frank asked him to clarify his name once again, as if Frank had misunderstood him. The man repeated the same name, "My name is Joel Garcia." Frank, startled with surprise, started to yell in excitement over in my direction of what he had just heard. So he called me over to meet the man. Frank mentioned we shared the same exact name and introduced me as, "This is Pastor Joel Garcia." We marveled at this encounter. So I shook his hand, made small talk, and eventually left since we had more food boxes to give away. I was in awe too—what a coincidence, I thought to myself at first.

Moments later, as we drove past the man's house, we saw he was still working in his garage. This time, I noticed he was welding a gate together out of iron bars. I saw the sparks from the welding touch light up the garage inside. I did not think much about it until later in the afternoon. After the outreach, I was relaxing on my couch at home, contemplating the successful event. While I sat there reflecting upon the wonderful outreach, I finally got the revelation God was attempting to convey to me. I thought to myself, "This whole encounter with the man named Joel was a **prophetic confirmation**."

On previous training occasions with my team, I would often mention to my team members, saying, "We have the privilege of building a *gate in the South* part of the city to establish God's kingdom." I said it so often that the church eventually took on a sub-name: ICLV—Southgate (Today, it's known as the ICLV—Dream Center). This prophetic encounter was simply a way **the Holy Spirit confirmed the prophetic word** spoken over my wife and I several years ago that we would go to the "south" and plant an extension for a short period of time.

After the outreach, the interpretation many of us also received from this testimony was summed up this way, "Joel Garcia is already in the South building a gate for God's kingdom." I was bewildered by this whole encounter. You cannot make this stuff up. This was truly an unusual sign from God. My wife and I knew then we were in the right "lane" in our lives, doing what God wanted us to do in this particular season of our lives.

> "Every good and perfect gift is from above, coming down
> from the Father of the heavenly lights, who does not change
> like shifting shadows."
> — James 1:17

God had spoken a prophetic word over my wife and I, and it took several years before it manifested. God sees beyond our limited "time in space" to bring us into His plans for our future. A **prophetic confirmation** like this one emboldened us to continue the work of the ministry without any lingering doubt our mind. It strengthened our spiritual resolve and fortitude. I noted this prophetic fulfillment as being the right time in my life to do what he called me to do. So I put my hands on the plow and did not look back.

Prophecy in a Time-Capsule:
The Cry of a Baby

In 1999, during the same conference, the late Prophet Cathy also added a second prophetic word to the prophecy, "And, I hear a cry of a baby in your home." Now, you must understand something, our children were already 14, 13, and 11 years of age. We were not looking to have another baby. In addition, the premise of having another child was inconceivable since I had a hysterectomy right after our third child was born in 1988. So, there was no possibility of my wife conceiving. So, I pondered this prophecy in my heart for sometime.

Now, our son has had a rough patch for several years in substance abuse. It lasted for 10 years, from the time he was sixteen to twenty-six years of age. My wife and I went through a gauntlet of struggle and misery, wondering if our son would survive the substance abuse. At sixteen, he ran away from home, thinking he could make it on his own by selling drugs on the streets. He went into a place of rebellion.

Six years later, he met a girl, and they both became addicted to drugs. Within time, they had a baby. Our mind had not connected the two previous prophecies together until a minor glitch happened right after the baby was born. Since both of them were addicted to drugs, the baby had some complications for the first 30 days after birth and was kept in the hospital's ICU unit. It should be obvious to you by now as to "why?" After sometime in the hospital, the baby eventually went home with the mother and her parents since they were not living together at the time. But for reasons I cannot discuss now, my wife and I eventually got custody of the baby.

You won't believe what happened next?

Now, fast track seven years later to 2006, where one morning I had a vivid dream. In the dream, I actually saw an infant in diapers in between my wife and I, and the baby was crying. I woke up from my dream since it was so vivid in nature, meaning it seemed so real it was impressed upon me. I remember waking up my wife and saying, "I had a dream about a baby in our bed." Now, we both connected this dream to the previous prophecy about "the sound of a child crying in our bed." The dream kept the mystery alive within us as we pondered both prophecies together. In the future months and years, we will bring up this prophecy in our conversations and pray about it.

On the first night, when the baby spent the night in our home, my wife and I heard "**the cry of a baby in our home**." The **prophecy was fulfilled** exactly as the prophet spoke. The tears just streamed down our faces, realizing how good God actually is to us—He forewarns us of a baby in our future. We never disbelieved the word; we just didn't know how it would end. The child lived with us for one full year, from six months to eighteen months. We watched her grow from the crawling stage to walking and to running around all over our house.

_____

_____

_____

_____

Diagram G:
Prophecy in Time-Capsule

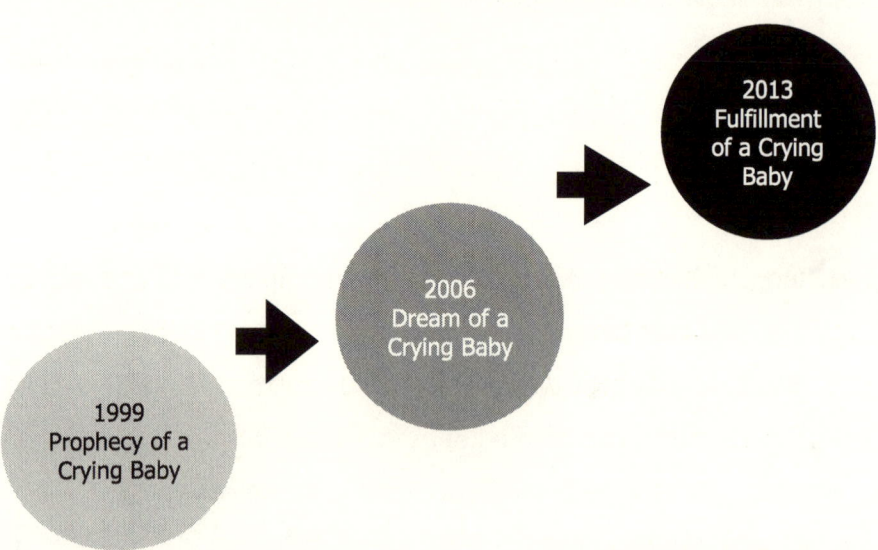

God abides outside of time, therefore, He sees the whole picture in time. We are given bits and pieces of the prophecy over time until it is fulfilled. This is why faith is so critical in time. The issue most of us have with prophecy is the "waiting time" for it to be fulfilled. To understand prophecy, we have to be patient and wait for its fulfillment, which is why we should not despise prophecy.[12]

When receiving a prophetic word, we should actually follow Mary's example by treating the prophecy like a "treasure." Therefore, we must "ponder" the prophecy (the treasure) in our heart.[13] The word

---

[12] 1 Thessalonians 5:20
[13] Luke 2:19

ponder means to throw together, hence; to discuss, consider, meet with it.[14] We must steward the prophetic word by a growing faith.

From my example, did you notice how after I received the dream, I connected the two prophecies together and after I had received the dream, I discussed it with my wife. In the ensuing days thereafter, I kept on pondering these two prophecies and considered what they meant in my life.

Prophecy sometimes is like connecting prophetic puzzle pieces together, and over time, you can see the intentions of God's heart for your life. Your prophetic word, through a process of time, is a test of your faithful stewardship.

> "Do not despise prophecies, but test everything; hold fast to what is good." — 1 Thessalonians 5:20-1-21 (ESV)

_____

_____

_____

_____

_____

_____

---

[14] Strong's Concordance: 4820 Sumballó; accessed online
https://biblehub.com/greek/4820.htm

| Section #5 | God's Multi-faceted Nature: God is Omnivident: He is All— Seeing |

God wants you to see what He sees; after all, we are made in His image and after His likeness. We can see in the dark places because God has allowed His Spirit to dwell within us. Therefore, we too can possess what is revealed about God in the scriptures. In the passages of Psalm 139:11-18, God reveals three things He wants you to know, they are:

1. **The Hidden Enemy** (Psalm 139:11-12): God wants you to peer into the darkness, so the enemy and his strategies against your life can be revealed and defeated.

2. **Your Hidden Identity** (Psalm 139: 13-16): God wants you to see yourself the way He designed you—they way He sees you, so you can know who you are in Christ.

3. **Your Hidden Destiny** (Psalm 139:16-18) God wants you to peek into the book in heaven so you can know the plans God has for your life, plans to give you hope and purpose.

I had not even heard of the word "omnivident" until I started to prep for a prophetic workshop. It was quite interesting to discover the word *omnivident* after 40 years as a Christian. I had known God as an omnipotent (all—powerful), omnipresent (all—present), and omniscient (all—knowing), but not an Omnivident, an "all—seeing" God. When I discovered this new facet of God's nature, I started to think about the animals who are nocturnal in nature, who hunt and eat at night. These nocturnal animals can see in the dark to hunt for prey. Among some of the animals who can see at night are some fowl, like owls; cats, and foxes. According to an Animal Science online periodical:

> "Nocturnal animals have more rods than daytime animals. The rods pick up light and help the animal see when it is almost completely dark outside. Many animals eyes have a special part called a tapetum lucidum. The tapetum lucidum helps with night vision. It is made of thick reflective cells and is beneath the retina."[15]

These animals require no light or the slightest presence of light from the stars or the moon to activate their night vision. The Bible notes, "God is light"[16] and "God dwells the unapproachable light."[17] Because

---

[15] Some Animals Can See in the Dark: Animal Science.
https://animalsmart.org/kids%27-zone/nocturnal-animals, accessed on 2/7/2023
[16] 1 John 1:5
[17] 1 Timothy 6:16

God is light, He doesn't not require a special lens for night vision like the creatures of night require to see in the dark. You will be able to see how God's night vision plays out in Psalm 139:11 & 12 in the next section, and how you can see in dark places.

God's Omnivident Power:

Psalm 139:11-18

God is omnivident; meaning nothing limits His vision; neither the brightness of light nor darkness.[18] Omnividence [noun] is the quality of being all-seeing.[19] This section of the outline for Psalm 139 enlightens us about the nature of God's visual prowess.

Let's read these verses to familiarize ourselves with this nocturnal vision:

11

If I say, "Surely the darkness will hide me, and the light become night around me,"

12

even the darkness will not be dark to you; the night will shine like the day, for darkness is as light to you.

13

For you created my inmost being; you knit me together in my mother's womb.

---

[18] Omnivident (Adjective) Wiktionary
[19] Omnividence (Noun) Wiktionary

14

I praise you because I am fearfully and wonderfully made;
your works are wonderful, I know that full well.

15

My frame was not hidden from you when I was made in the secret
place, when I was woven together in the depths of the earth.

16

Your eyes saw my unformed body; all the days ordained for me
were written in your book before one of them came to be.

17

How precious to me are your thoughts, oh God! How vast is the
sum of them!

18

Were I to count them, they would outnumber the grains of sand—
when I awake, I am still with you.

God can see in the darkness, which is why David mentioned, "the night will shine as the day, for darkness is as light to you." God can even see into a mother's womb, where life is initially conceived and develops until the day of delivery. We too can see into the darkness by the light of God. Allow me to share two stories from my own experience with night vision to explain this phenomena. I have more stories to offer, but these two incidents will suffice to make my point about grooming a **prophetic night lens**—the ability to see into the darkness, much like God does.

1. God Wants You to See into the Darkness, So You can See and Defeat the Hidden Enemy

Nocturnal Encounters: Prophetic Visions in the Night

God wants us to be more like Him. Therefore, he desires to show you the hidden enemy. God wants to open your eyes so you can see in the darkness. An enemy that cannot be seen cannot be defeated. An enemy that is revealed to you is an enemy you can see and defeat. What is the secret formula for your eyes to be opened to see in the darkness? First, you are children of light, light already resides within you. Second, if you desire to see in the darkness, like God does, so you can see and defeat the hidden enemy, then apply the **A.S.K.** principle to your prayer life:

— **Ask**: Pray and ask God for this gift to be released into your life.

— **Seek**: Continue seeking after this gift by reading scriptures that are aligned with seeing, vision, night visions and light; Joshua 9, Acts 13:4—12, and many others.

— And **knock**: Keep knocking on heaven's door. God will then see your passion and give you what you have been asking for. Read: Hebrews 4:16.

The Ninja Demon:
A Demonic Shadow in the Darkness of Night

One early morning within the past year, I fell asleep on the couch in the family room after watching a movie. All of a sudden, around 1:30 am, my spiritual eyes were opened, and I saw a shadow next to me. Yes, you heard me right. In the darkness of the night, I detected a shadow next to me. It was looking me up and down like it was examining me. "How can this happen?" I thought to myself. How can a person see a shadow in the darkness of the night? Night vision helps you to discern and separate darkness from darkness. King David states in Psalm 139:11-12:

> "If I say, 'Surely the darkness will hide me and the light become night around me,' even the darkness will not be dark to you; the night will shine like the day, for darkness is as light to you."

Occult means "hidden,"— Revelation means to "unveil."
God desires to unveil (or reveal) the hidden enemy so you can triumph!

Some time ago, I read this scripture; I began to ask God to give me this "night-time vision," very much like God's vision to see into the night. This was the second time my spirit eyes had opened to see in the darkness of the night. Since then I have experienced this several times over. What I saw that night was the shadow of a demon. I was not frightened, nor was I worried about its presence next to me, when my sprit-eyes supernaturally opened to see it. When you are able to see a demon, you have authority and power over it. As soon as I saw it, I commanded it "to leave my presence 'in the name of Jesus.'" Then, I leaned back peaceably upon my pillow to regain my sleep. Just before I returned to my sleep, something unusual happened outside my house.

Now, within a minute or so, as I was going back to sleep, I heard a man's voice in the street, in front of my house, in deep sorrow and grief, like he was deeply disappointed about something. The man-made incoherent and weeping sounds, and then the voice disappeared down the street. The Lord then revealed to me the man who designed the witchcraft against me had been exposed. The man who had sent the Ninja demon in my direction, his most secret weapon, had received a seven-fold return as punishment and was deeply troubled by it to the point of weeping and deep sorrow.

Student Exercise:

For three months, at least, in moments of rest right before bedtime, close your eyes. You will be able to see points of light coming in, such as a dot of light or images of light. Focus upon one of these points of light and follow it as long as you can. Try to enlarge the light, to look deeper into heaven's portal. Keep doing this over and over a few times each night, and over a period of time, the Holy Spirit and you will train your spirit to see in the darkness.

The point of this exercise is to train your spiritual eye-gate, and to enlarge the scope of your night vision. The Holy Spirit takes note of your faith and will honor you for it, by opening up your spiritual lens to see more clearly in the dark.

Why We Need to See into the Dark Realms?

As the people of light, you should be aware of the enemy's schemes over your life, your loved ones, and strategies over your city. In a sense, you become a Watchman or Watch-woman over your home, over your family, and your city. Isaiah, the prophet, notes:

> "No weapon that is fashioned against you shall prosper, and you shall confute every tongue that rises against you in judgment. This is the heritage of the servants of the Lord and their vindication from me, says the Lord."
> — Isaiah 54:17 (NRSV)

Being able to have "night vision" is the ability to go into the enemy's camp to see what he is doing (revelation), so we, through wisdom, can develop the strategies to thwart his plans through intercessory prayer, powerful decrees, and declarations. Prophet Chuck D. Pierce says, "Revelation dismantles demons, and revelation with wisdom unseats principalities." It's time to unseat principalities.

_____

_____

_____

_____

_____

_____

_____

_____

2. God Wants to Reveal Your Hidden Identity

God Can See Into a Mother's Womb

God's omnivident power is able to see not only in the darkness like we do in the daytime, but He can also see into a mother's womb. What can be more obscure than a mother's womb? Modern science finally made a breakthrough with the Fetal Ultrasound device, which is able to see through a woman's abdomen, through the lining of the skin, and through the thick placenta to probe deeply within to bring up images of a developing child in picture form upon a screen. Parents today are able to see their children through technology. However, before technology ever made such advances, God gave David a revelation, in picture form, into the developmental process of a child in the mother's womb.

We, like David, were knitted and woven in our mother's womb, according to Psalm 139:13. How did David know we were "woven" (or knitted)? The word *woven* in Hebrew is a picture of a woman knitting a garment. The process of knitting is an intricate stitching process where two pieces are attached, merging together to solidify into one garment. David was given a vision of how DNA is bonded together to create a human being, which is why David said, "I am fearfully and wonderfully made; I know that full well." When David saw this miraculous process taking place through a revelation, he was astounded of God's marvelous works.

God is able to see the process of life being formed in a womb, from the starting phases of conception through the child's full development, even to the natural process of giving birth.

This is why David said:

15

My frame was not hidden from you when I was made in the secret place,
when I was woven together in the depths of the earth.

16

Your eyes saw my unformed body;
all the days ordained for me were written in your book
before one of them came to be.

17

Your eyes saw my unformed body;
all the days ordained for me were written in your book
before one of them came to be.

God knows you so well. His involvement and oversight of the formation of your life and body in your mother's womb only shows you how much He is in tune with your life, from beginning to end. Your life, however, was written in eternity before you were even conceived, according to verse 17b above.

_____

_____

A Prophetic Word of Restoration

My daughter had lost a child in her womb several months into her pregnancy. My daughter and her husband were devastated by the incident, and so were my wife and I. Several months later, we attended the Prophetic Conference at our church, where Prophet Jim Laffoon was the speaker. During the altar time, He called my wife and I, along with my daughter, who was in attendance in the service to the stage. Prophet Lagoon prophesied over my wife and I. Then, it was my daughter's turn to receive a prophetic word. The prophet greeted my daughter and began to speak a prophetic word over her life. At the time, my daughter was pregnant again, and we did not know it. She withheld from tellings us the good news since she wanted to wait until after the baby's first trimester. Here's a partial sample of the prophetic word spoken over her life:

> "... Daughter you love me, you are passionate about me... says the Lord... but you and your husband tried to figure out what to do with the dream that seemed to die."

At this point, she began to cry and placed her hands over her face.

> "I want to remind you of the Shumanite woman, remember
> her, the prophet said, 'Come up, you gonna have a child.' She
> said, 'Don't hurt me Lord, don't hurt me.' ...
> And, just when she [The Shumanite woman] was getting
> ready to reap, it died. You were like, 'My husband and I were
> just getting to reap and it died.'"

At this moment, she *bent over and started to shake* because of the
raw pain from the trauma still residing within her. It was the
penetrating voice of God going deep into her vat, delivering her from
the trauma and pain. The prophet continued:

> "'It died and [you] did not know what to do. Your husband is
> a great man, but it injured him too... it knocked the wind out
> of his sails too... and you did not know how to recover... Now
> you love me and you were raised to love me. Sometimes faith
> feels like you are going through the motions... I am so proud
> you stayed faithful... the Lord says, I want you to know I am
> the resurrection and the life... A *second wind and touch* is
> coming to a dream... a second dream and touch. You are good
> parents says the Lord. I am coming back, says the Lord, to
> give you 'pressed down, a good measure, and flowing over'
> (Luke 6:38)...this is a new day!'" [Italics are mine]

Can you imagine the joy that filled our hearts over this prophetic
word? Soon, days after the service, our daughter confided in us that
she was pregnant again. That same year, in late September, she gave
birth to a girl. I want you to know something, the scripture from Luke
6:38 was the portion of the prophecy delivered over this baby's life.

Diagram H:
A "Time-Travel" Prophecy

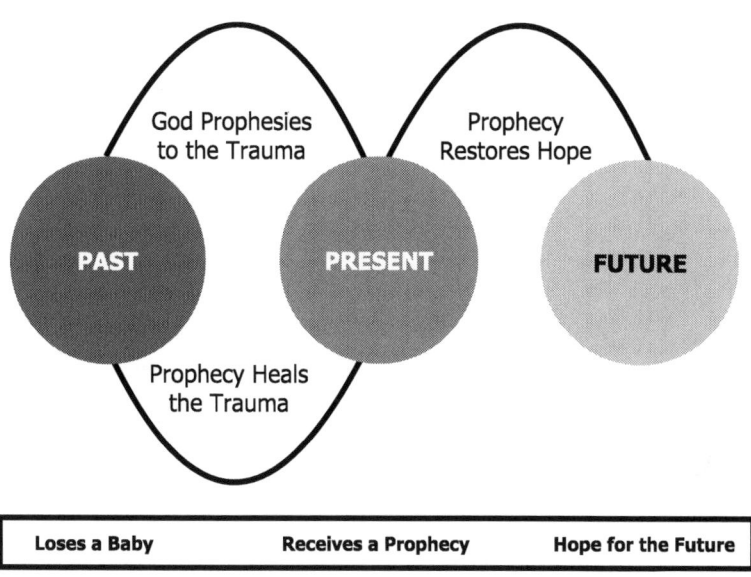

Loses a Baby	Receives a Prophecy	Hope for the Future

The prophetic word came to pass over her life. Today, the child is filled with an overflowing personality, fulfilling the scripture given over her life of being "pressed down, a good measure and flowing over." She lives out his scripture every day of her life. As soon as she walks into a room, her personality takes over and fills the room with energy and joy. She is definitely a bundle of joy to have in our lives.

Do you see how God first goes back in time to heal trauma, then provides a prophetic word in the present filled with hope for a better future?

3. God Wants to Reveal Your Hidden Destiny

The Book of Life: Reaching Your Full Potential

> "For I know the plans I have for you," declares the LORD, "plans to prosper you and not to harm you, plans to give you hope and a future."
> — Jeremiah 29:11 (NIV)

Your life is a mystery, an unfolding story revealed through time. The purpose of prophecy is to discover what is written in this book about your life so you can access the gems and live out your prophetic destiny. The third reason why God desires to open your eyes with His light is to reveal your life's purpose and destiny so you can reach your full potential.

David mentions a "book of your life" in Psalm 139:17b, where "the days ordained for me were written in your book before one of them came to be." God has your best life written out for you.

Can you imagine, God has a book, a script about your best God-ordained life already written in eternity?

So what's the purpose of this book in heaven anyway?

If you think you get the full picture of your life given to you all at once, you are misguided. God releases portions of the drama of your life in portions, as you walk in intimacy with Him. You just have to get to know Him, abide in Him, and ask to get a glimpse into that book from time to time.

The reason why you need a special kind of lens to see in the dark and, for the most part, to be able to see your life's purpose in the eternal book is so you can access all that God has for you. Prophecy reveals what is hidden in that book through a relationship with the Father.

Can you imagine, getting to heaven one day and only being able to see that you only fulfilled 25% of what was written about you in the eternal book? What would you say to yourself?

_____

_____

_____

_____

_____

_____

This is why prophecy plays a role in revealing what's in the Book of Life for your life. Its time to embrace the prophetic ministry, so you can start to unfold God's plan for your life!

_____

_____

_____

_____

_____

_____

Appendix A | Discovering My Prophetic Code Language

Moses' Prophetic Code Language: Face—to—Face with God

Moses had a prophetic code language—it was a face—to—face encounter and communication with a loving God. Moses' first encounter came through a "burning-bush," which burned before him (face-to-face) but was not consumed by the fire. Moses called it a "strange sight." This same fire can live within us through Christ. God's presence can burn within us without fulling consuming us. Moses had other face—to—face encounters with the Living God. Much later, when some rivals became jealous of Moses' relationship with God, God said:

> "Listen to my words: 'When there is a prophet among you, I, the LORD, reveal myself to them in visions, I speak to them in dreams. But this is not true of my servant Moses; he is faithful in all my house. With him I speak **face to face**, clearly and not in riddles; he sees the form of the LORD.'"
> — Numbers 12:6-9

God chose to speak to Moses in a certain way. Moses had his own prophetic code language. In this passage, it is also noted how he spoke to other prophets of the time through visions, dreams, and riddles. They had a prophetic code language of their own. God will choose the manner of speaking to you. God has a code language just for you. We just need to discover it for ourselves!

How do you discover your prophetic code language? It will take several prophetic encounters before you begin to understand how God speaks to you.

What is Your Prophetic Code Language?

Check off the ones you feel are more frequent than others, then rate the frequency of each one by a scale of 1-10.

PROPHETIC CATEGORY & RATING

(Scale: 1-3 Weak / 4-6 Moderate / 7-10 Strong)

Mark	Spiritual	Senses	Rating
	Seeing		
_____	Images	_____	
_____	Patterns	_____	
_____	Pictures	_____	
_____	Repetitions	_____	
_____	Sequences	_____	
_____	Symbols	_____	
_____	Colors	_____	

Mark	Hearing	Rating
_____	Audible Voice	_____
_____	Penetrating Voice	_____
_____	Still Small Voice	_____

Mark	Smelling	Rating
_____	Perfumes	_____
_____	Fruits	_____
_____	Stenches	_____
_____	Smells of childhood	_____

Mark	Tasting	Rating
_____	Palette	_____

Mark	Feeling/Touch	Rating
_____	Impressions	_____

Mark	Dreams	Rating
_____	Vivid Dreams	_____
_____	Stirring Dreams	_____

Mark	Visions	Rating
_____	Day Visions	_____
_____	Night Visions	_____

Mark	Other	Rating
_____	Wisdom of others	_____
_____	Circumstances	_____
_____	Holy Spirit: Rhema	_____
_____	Jesus: Logos	_____
_____	Trance	_____
_____	Angels	_____

Can you list any other way God has spoken to you or others not listed in this assessment?

_____

_____

_____

_____

According to your assessment, your top 3 dominant ways God speaks to you to capture your attention are:

1._____

2. _____

3. _____

These three areas consist of you prophetic code language God uses on a more regular basis to speak to you. There are many ways God can convey a prophetic message to you, but these three are your prominent areas of prophetic revelation.

_____

_____

_____

_____

_____

_____

Appendix B | The 3 Stages of Processing a Prophetic Algorithm

Stage 1: <u>Detecting</u> a Prophetic Algorithm

In Acts 10:9—16, Peter received a prophetic revelation as he rested on the rooftop of the Tanner's house.

a. The revelation came in the form of a **trance**—a visual cinema before him with unforgettable images and meanings and a voice with instructions.

— Do you remember what a "trance" is?

— Have you ever had a spiritual trance?

b. Peter **interacted** with the prophetic revelation each time—"Not me Lord, I have never eaten anything unclean."
— Peter knew it was the Lord who was speaking to him.
— Peter, at first, resisted the idea of eating outside his prescribed diet.

What else do you see in the narrative?

c. The prophetic revelation was released three times in a **sequence of similar patterns and repetitions.**

— Can you list the patterns, repetitions and sequences? If not, go back and review pages 39-40.

Stage 2: <u>Discerning & Deciphering</u> a Prophetic Algorithm

a. **Discerning** a prophetic algorithm in Acts 10:17-20:

"Now while Peter **wondered** within himself what this vision which he had seen meant, behold, the men who had been sent from Cornelius house, and stood at the gate." (— Acts 10:17 NKJV)

The word **"wondered"** (diaporeo; Strongs G1280) means: "to be entirely at a loss; to be in perplexity."

— Peter, at this time, is beginning to **discern** the prophetic algorithm. Revelation, at times, will be perplexing when it comes in multiple layers, which means you need to go a step further.

b. **Deciphering** a prophet algorithm in Acts 10:17-20

"While Peter **thought** about the vision, the Spirit said to him, 'Behold, three men are seeking you. Arise, therefore, go down and go with them, doubting nothing for I have sent them.'" (— Acts 10:19, 20 NKJV)

The word **"thought"** (enthymeomai; Strongs G1760) means: "to consider deeply."

Note: Peter took his thoughts a step further, from being perplexed to deeply considering the revelation he had received.

— We must take the time to delve deeper into the prophecy to decipher its meaning!

_____

_____

_____

Stage 3: Attaining the __Direct Outcome__ of a Prophetic Algorithm

Every prophetic algorithm, once you have adjudicated it as coming from God, will have a purpose for you to execute.

If you, by faith, walk out the prophetic algorithm to completion, you will soon decipher the algorithm much like Peter did with Cornelius.

__Direct Outcome__:

When did Peter know this prophetic algorithm had run its course?

"Then Peter began to speak: 'I now realize how true it is that God does not show favoritism but accepts from every nation the one who fears him and does what is right.'" — Acts 10:34-35 NIV

The prophetic algorithm had successfully run its course!

_____

_____

_____

_____

_____

_____

_____

_____

_____

_____

Appendix C

The Shamar Anointing: Two Encounters for Discerning and Deciphering a Prophetic Algorithm at Night-time

Read each encounter to help you assess a prophetic algorithm from start to finish. Let's see if you can find the components of **detecting, discerning and deciphering and its direct outcome:**

Prophetic Encounter #1:
The Rattling of Door Knob

I came home one night around 11:00 pm, and I stayed up for a bit before going to bed. I went to bed around midnight, then, in the early morning hour, around 1:30 am, two and a half hours later, I was awakened by a vivid dream. In the dream, I felt someone was breaking into my home, as I heard a sound like someone was rattling the knob of one of my doors. The feeling was so strong, so I woke up from my sleep, got out of my bed, and went to check all my entry doors. One of the last things I do before going to bed, I make my rounds around the house to ensure all the doors are locked and secure any open windows.

At first, I thought, "Did I secure my doors?" So I got up to check each door, starting from the sliding glass door at the rear of the house to the front door and, finally, the door leading out to the garage. All the doors were locked. So, I paused, then thought to myself, "I must have left the garage door opened." So I unlocked the door and went out into the garage. To my surprise, guess what I discovered? I left my car on—it was still running. My wife's car has one of those keyless ignitions, where the engine is silent when its on idle. I must have gotten distracted by something before getting out of the car. After turning the car off, I thought to myself:

> "The dream wasn't about someone trying to break into my home. It was the Holy Spirit trying to break into my sleep."

The dream stirred me out of my sleep with enough concern just to get me out of bed to do a thorough check of my home. God had spoken to me through the rattling of a door knob. Honestly, I don't know what would have happened if I had left the car on all night until morning. All I know is God watches over me. He is the Watchman over my family and home. The Bible clearly states:

> "Unless the LORD builds the house, those who build it labor in vain. Unless the   LORD watches over the city, the watchman stays awake in vain."[20]

The gist of the scripture is simply this: If we build anything without His approval, we strive in its development and construction. When the night guard tries to watch over the city, he does so in vain, if God is not with him.

---

[20] Psalm 127:1 (BSB)

I'm so thankful God is with me!

Your Thoughts:

_____

_____

_____

_____

_____

_____

_____

_____

_____

_____

_____

_____

_____

_____

_____

_____

_____

_____

Prophetic Encounter #2:

Closing an Open Door

I have spent the night at a family member's house several times over the years when they have somewhere to go for the weekend. Not all the time, but some of the times my wife and I have spent the night, I have noticed some of the children do not sleep very well. They toss and turn and, at times, cry out to their parents. There have been times I would just walk over to sleep on the floor in their bedroom so they know someone is nearby. In the past, I have always felt some witchcraft going on around their neighborhood. How do I know? You can feel it—my sleep is not the same. I get disturbed at odd times in the night. Knowing this ahead of time, on my next trip,[21] I decided to be more spiritually aware and to pay closer attention to the signs. In addition, I was determined to get up to pray and watch this time. These is called a "prayer watch" where you take time to pray, worship, and intercede on behalf of others. This is also a time of silence to be still and listen to what God is saying. The purpose is to pick up on the subtle nuances of the prophetic voice of God and allow Him to spotlight the issues.

During the first night, in my sleep, I heard the sound of a door opening. So I got up to check the house. As usual, all the doors were locked, so I knew it was a demonic attempt to enter the house. So I got up and just started to worship God. I did this for a period of time. I wanted His presence to fill the home. I wanted Him to occupy it. I then asked God to secure the perimeter of the house and all the entryways. This way, I invite Him to be the Watchman over the

---

[21] October 21-23rd 2022.

house. Soon after, I felt God's peace over me, so I decided to go back to bed. That night, my grandchildren did not make a sound; they slept peacefully throughout the rest of the night.

The next night, however, I heard a sound like someone was trying to get in through the front door. The door jostled with a sound like someone was trying to get in, but they did not have access since the night before, I took spiritual authority to secure the perimeter of the house. That night, I decreed over and over, "No weapon formed against me or my family will prosper."[22] I was doing spiritual and prophetic warfare over my family and their house; decreeing and declaring peace over the house. I now knew a demonic presence was being sent by someone in the neighborhood into my family's house to disturb the sleep of my grandchildren, and do other diabolical things.

On our third and final night of the weekend, nothing significant happened other than I asked God to "reveal the person" causing the demonic intrusion into the home. I knew God would tell me. Well, the first night back home in Las Vegas, I had a dream of a couple in the neighborhood. I had met them in the past, and they both seemed like nice neighbors. In the dream, I found myself hidden in the bed of my son-in-law's truck outside in the driveway, being the Watchman of the neighborhood. All of a sudden, I saw the man come out of a house with five youth. All of the youth were dressed in hip-hop outfits (baggy) with beanies on their heads covering their identity. Three of them went into what seemed like a door, entering the garage, and two of them stayed outside. The two youth outside held their hands

---

[22] Isaiah 54:17

up in the air. Much like they were giving up to the authorities (the spiritual authority in the neighborhood). All of a sudden, a car drove up, picked them up, and left the neighborhood. The older man of the home was present, holding what seemed to be a training manual of some kind. Then, the older man and his wife started to walk back to their home. At one point, the older man looked over his right shoulder and saw me peeking at him from the bed of the truck. I then ducked my head in the bed of the truck, but I knew he saw me. He leaned over to his wife and alerted her of my presence. Now they both knew who I was too.

Once you receive a prophetic warning or prompting (Revelation means unveiling), it allows you to see the hidden things (Occult means hidden). If you can see in the spirit, then you have the spiritual authority to do something about it. Therefore, exert your spiritual authority to "bind the kingdom of darkness and to lose the kingdom of light" in the atmosphere. Take authority and reclaim the atmosphere in your home from the enemy and allow God to possess it with His presence.

Your Thoughts:

_____

_____

_____

_____

_____

_____

Appendix D | A Glossary of Prophetic Terms and Symbols

As a prophetic intercessor, you will clash with the kingdom of darkness from time to time. This glossary is a list of prophetic terms and symbols that were acquired from my own revelatory experiences over the last few years (2021—2023):

Blood Sucking Demons: At a last-ditch effort, these demons are sent to take a blood sample of you and your bloodline. The purpose is to see what iniquities or weaknesses are in your bloodline so new strategies can be developed. Demons hate letting go of your bloodline.

Buer: The Great President of Hell, who has 50 legions of demons under its command. The Romans considered a group of 5,000 soldiers a legion. If you multiply 5,000 soldiers into 50 legions, you arrive at a figure of two—hundred & fifty—thousand demons under its command.

This demonic principality is a hybrid of a spider's body with a distorted man's face and head, which spins its head around the neck socket depending on its position on the wall, ceiling, or the ground.

Demonic Portals: Demons enter through portals to depress, oppress, and suppress people. Although they are spirit beings who can enter by any means, we often see them in our dreams entering or exiting through doors, windows, vents, toilets, sinks, shower drains, and even electrical wiring. This is God's way of showing you how they enter and warning you an intruder is present. You have the authority to seal the breaches in your home. So get up and do something about it!

Dog Sniffing Demons: A dog-sniffing demon comes around you to sniff out a scent from you. If you have compromised yourself in some way, these "dog-sniffing demons" will find the scent and trace it to the origin of your compromise. They are trying to find an open door in your life so they can take advantage of that open—door.

Electrical Portals: Portals are spiritual entryways the demonic uses to enter a home. Demons use electrical systems to gain access to your home. You have authority over your home to close these portals of demonic insurgency and activity.

Helen, the Principality (or goddess) of Beauty and War: This female principality operates over Las Vegas to keep men and women in bondage to sexual pleasures so they can be subdued, manipulated, and defenseless in the spiritual warfare battle. This principality is known as the Greek "goddess of beauty and the goddess of war," who seduces men's souls through lust, sexual addiction, etc.

Ninja Demon: These demons cloaked themselves in dark clothing in the darkness of the night. They blend into dark environments at night, so you cannot see nor detect them. However, as people of light with enlightened spiritual eyes (read Section 4) you can separate darkness from darkness and discern their presence. The Ninja Demon is the hidden enemy God wants you to see and defeat.

Light Portals—Specs of Light: When you close your eyes, you can see specs of light. These are portals and/or angelic beings. There are times when the light becomes so evident in my life I can see angelic and demonic activity, images, and unknown people's faces.

Prophetic Algorithm: The word *algorithm, a* term from the tech world, is the "process or set of rules to be followed in calculations or other problem-solving operations, especially by a computer." Common examples include: the recipe for baking a cake, the method we use to solve a long division problem, and the process of doing laundry are all examples of an algorithm.

A *prophetic algorithm* encompasses the total process from revelation, delivered by single or multiple sensory devices, to arrive at God's prophetic intent. We apply this methodology of solving prophecy: detection + discerning / deciphering = direct outcome.

Prophetic Code Language: This is your own personal style of receiving revelation from God. Moses met with God "face—to—face." If you read the book of Acts, the Apostle Paul leans more "nocturnal," in receiving prophetic revelation. There are four times Paul had received night visions and visitations. Our prophetic code language is determined by our receptivity to certain spiritual algorithms, more than other forms.

For example, I tend to receive revelation in vivid dreams in the early morning hours, through my five spiritual senses and night visions and visitations.

Prophetic Confirmation: A prophetic confirmation is when a prophetic word has an unquestionable sign following, which confirms and validates the authenticity of the prophetic word spoken over your life.

Appendix E | My Prophetic Journal

Prophetic Algorithm Journal: Incident #1   Date: _____

Describe a Prophetic Algorithm: The types of multi-sensory applications used

_____

_____

_____

_____

Discern & Decipher the Prophetic Algorithm: Break it down

_____

_____

_____

_____

Describe God's Prophetic Intent: What was God conveying to you?

_____

_____

_____

_____

Prophetic Algorithm Journal: Incident #2   Date: _____

Describe a Prophetic Algorithm: The Types of Multi-sensory Applications

_____

_____

_____

_____

_____

Discern & Decipher the Prophetic Algorithm: Break it Down

_____

_____

_____

_____

_____

Describe God's Prophetic Intent:

_____

_____

_____

_____

_____

Prophetic Algorithm Journal: Incident #3   Date: _____

Describe Prophetic Algorithm: The Types of Multi-sensory Applications

_____

_____

_____

_____

_____

Discern & Decipher the Prophetic Algorithm: Break it Down

_____

_____

_____

_____

_____

Describe God's Prophetic Intent: What was God conveying to you?

_____

_____

_____

_____

_____

Prophetic Algorithm Journal: Incident #4   Date: _____

Describe a Prophetic Algorithm: The Types of Multi-sensory Applications

_____

_____

_____

_____

_____

Discern & Decipher the Prophetic Algorithm: Break it Down

_____

_____

_____

_____

_____

Describe God's Prophetic Intent: What was God conveying to you?

_____

_____

_____

_____

_____

About Us: Marketplace Mastery — Global Training Center

"Doing Business with Spirit"

We are a premier prophetic school of ministry for entrepreneurs, small business leaders, and busy professionals who desire to manifest the manifold wisdom of God in the marketplace. Simply put, we equip business leaders for marketplace ministry, business development, and transformational leadership.

We accomplish our objective by first offering a specific slate of kingdom-centric curricula designed to align faith-based leaders with the global imperative found in Matthew 28:18-20 and Ephesians 4:11—13. The Great Commission and the Discipleship Model provide the Christian business leader with a clear and direct imperative to "Go and make disciples of all nations." We believe the business sphere is a "nation" all of its own with a distinct set of rules, language, and culture. The business sphere is considered one of the seven mountains of culture.

We are committed to making disciples in the marketplace with a transformational mindset. Our courses are offered online or live each week, and they are delivered in English and in Spanish by top instructors. Upon graduation, our students receive the coveted Marketplace Minister's certificate and become a permanent staple of our marketplace tribe.

Business & Leadership Coaching and Consulting

In addition, we are a business consultancy agency committed to training and coaching Kingdom business leaders to adopt and apply Kingdom concepts to their everyday business practices and their personal and professional lives. As we shape kingdom leaders to prosper within their respective fields of business, we also believe each person can minister in the marketplace.

Business Lunches, Seminars and Conferences

We also gather believers through our yearly business conferences, quarterly seminars, and monthly B.O.A.Z. (Business Owners for Jesus) Lunch and Learns to enhance our brand among Kingdom-minded business leaders in the marketplace.

The Founder and Executive Director

In 2021, Joel C. Garcia, founded Marketplace Mastery — Global Training Center as an apostolic and prophetic ministry school for entrepreneurs, small business leaders and busy professionals to manifest the manifold wisdom of God in the marketplace.

Joel was an executive pastor at a large church for sixteen years, supervising different aspects of ministry operations, including Director of a Bible school, and a successful church plant. Joel then transitioned into the marketplace taking possession of key roles in top management positions in two financial businesses, and then as owner and operator of his own consulting firm and staffing agency. Joel's background, as a ministry and business leader, equipped him with a unique ability, and skill sets necessary to coach, mentor and train Christian entrepreneurs, small business owners, and top managers to thrive in their God-given sphere of authority in the marketplace.

In February of 2024, Joel received an Honorary degree of Doctor of Philosophy in Humanities from the United Graduate College and Seminary International, which is accredited under Worldwide Accreditation Commission of Christian Education (WWAC). Joel also holds a Master's of Organizational Leadership degree with an emphasis in coaching and mentoring from Regent University, located in Virginia Beach, Virginia.

As a result, Joel has written over a dozen books ranging from prophetic leadership to spiritual influence topics, and three workbooks geared to coaching business leaders on how to manifest the prophetic ministry in the marketplace.

Social Media:

You can follow, interact and contact us online through our social media platforms:

Facebook: @marketplacemastery

Instagram: @marketplace_mastery

Twitter: @mm_gtc

YouTube: @marketplacemastery

Website: www.mmgtc.com

2024, All Rights Reserved

Marketplace Mastery, GTC, llc.

Business Coaching, Prophetic Leadership

Made in the USA
Middletown, DE
17 March 2025

72734231R00072